Quest

121 questions of liberation
from the prison of self-domestication

Cristina Gallegos & John E. Kobara

Cover Art: *Meditation and the Egg,* by Tomi D. Kobara
Cover Design: Cristina Gallegos

ISBN: 979-8-3304-3154-0
Library of Congress Cataloging-in-Publication Data

WARNING

This book contains disruptive content which could dramatically and positively alter your point of view. Everything in here is true, except what we made up. You may encounter unnecessary amounts of hubris, shards of ego, some pasteurized preachiness or other artificial and synthetic ingredients that have been known to aggravate human subjects. The reader may experience symptoms of dizziness, hallucinations, vertigo, and in rare cases, self-awareness. Embarking on this Quest could be threatening to the life you are currently leading.

Awaken.

Awaken.

Yearn for the exceptional,

and mainstream it.

Not for others,

but for oneself.

Ignite,

self-immolate

in the brightness of you,

shake,

rejigger,

burn with a radical fire.

Be savage.

The world deserves nothing less.

You deserve nothing less.

From John…

To Sarah: I dedicate this book to you. For your unconditional love. For your indulgence of my quirks and habits. For your guidance in helping me become a better human, husband, parent, and writer.

To Jenna, Malia, and Bobby: You are the magic of the future. Your generous spirits, compassion, and energy give me hope. Thank you for laughing at me and with me. Happiness is being your father.

To Cristina: Thank you for being on this adventure with me. For pushing and pulling me to express myself.

To Tanya, always.

Start Here! Quick Guide

This is a book of 121 questions to transform your life.

- ✓ **Find an inquiry line that resonates:** Read in sequence, or flip through the book until one question rings right. Look at the table of contents <u>and the index</u>.

- ✓ **Read the question and its answers:** We have collected multigenerational perspectives to ignite your viewpoint. Agree or disagree. No right or wrong.

- ✓ **Answer the question!** You are the heart of this book. Your answer is the only thing of true substance.

- ✓ **Write! This is a writing book not a reading book:** The empty page after each question is a working space. Use extra paper if needed. Jot down anything, draw something. Stay silly, weird, be uncomfortable. <u>The more you dislike the question, the more useful it could prove.</u>

- ✓ **Use the Index as a guiding map:** We have clustered the questions into the "seasons" of life and categorized the questions based on dimensions such as IDENTITY, TIME, GOALS, PAIN, etc. to find what you may need.

- ✓ **Questions are evergreen:** Open the book and sit with it; stare at the blank space, let the heart speak. Your stage of life will shift the relevance of the impulse.

- ✓ **Squeeze value out of it:** We just gave you an Oracle fueled by your own life force. A special kind of Tarot to revisit and extract something new of value. It will always be right, and it will always be right there for you.

A guiding path

Be patient toward all that is unsolved in your heart and try to love the questions themselves, like locked rooms and books that are now written in a very foreign tongue. Do not seek the answers, which cannot be given to you because you would not be able to live them. And the point is, to live everything. Live the questions now. Perhaps you will then gradually, without noticing it, live along some distant day into the answer.

Rainier Maria Rilke

This quest is spiritual. It holds insights, a moment of pause, and, if the gods are kind, a positive shift. There's a chance that if you are reading this, you are hungry for some important answers.

We are most definitely neither gurus, nor gym trainers putting you through your paces. What we are known for, is poking provocatively, and serving rich morsels to chew on at length. *Quest* will show how much you have already decided in life, how thoroughly wonderful you actually are, and how much you still yearn to discover. Embarking on the journey will force the rethinking of assumptions. Stay curious. Unknowing and unlearning might follow, and we promise there will be some new gold once you are done with the book.

Although this volume might be angling for self-improvement, asking the questions is far from implying that anyone might be in need of fixing. We actually KNOW that you are already perfect. Our deepest hope is to push you to a point where you start to thoroughly believe that you are magnificent!

A perfect answer wrapped in certainty is not important. And while we have included a certain degree of directiveness, not everything will have an articulated takeaway. Our intention is to avoid spoon-feeding or pointing to how much spinning your centrifuge needs. The shared perspectives are meant more as case studies, and less as shiny points to contemplate. Feel free to do exactly the opposite of what you read.

The pages are ordered into seasons because humans often experience all weather at all times. Perspective-shifting, reflection, and asymmetry, are squarely intended as goals of the *Quest*. Know that circling around a given question could feel like walking past a painting in a museum. Maybe it says something, and maybe it doesn't. Maybe it hits you all of a sudden and something new is being seen. You will know.

The right questions will enter your life like the dance between the matador and the bull, both dancing under the music, for the benefit of the audience, with the specter of death hanging over their heads; a show, yes, but with blood on the line.

If you think you need clarifications, we are here to tell you that you don't. Just trust the question. The zinger is good. The *"ouch!"* is good. And so is the occasional discomfort. If at the end there's any mystery left, then we did well.

Now go!

Table of Contents

Spring

Summer

Fall

Winter

About us

Why should you listen to us? I mean, not that you have to listen to us, but it could save you time, some grief maybe, fluctuations in decision-making, and even money.

We live in an age where the village elders have been replaced by decaying truth on social media and polarized monologues in echo chambers. Having in your corner people who've been around the block once or twice can come in handy.

In writing this book, we decided to skip repeated references to our professional subject-matter expertise and spare you the drudgery of having to plow through too many hints of the Pygmalion-like chiseling hardships we each endured throughout the years. We will refrain from sharing an abundance of ego-filled distillations from our combined school of hard knocks and the various actual universities we have clawed our respective way through. Our backgrounds, professional successes, and personal achievements are important in one way, and one way only: because we want you to know that snake oil is not what we peddle, and that, at least on occasion, we might be a good temporary proxy for the aforementioned village elders you might not have. This is why we will share our story, but only once, and only here.

Who is John, you ask?

I am a provocateur. I am a facilitator of change. I am a conversationalist.

My family traces its roots to 1106, in 12th century feudal Japan, 36 generations from the first Shogun, Minamoto no Yoritomo.

I am proud of being a third generation Japanese-American. Whatever wisdom I share, comes from the dreams of my great-grandparents who were killed by the atomic bomb in Hiroshima, and from the hopes of my grandparents and parents, who were all imprisoned in the internment camps of Poston Arizona during World War II.

I acknowledge the great many gifts I have received from my DNA, and the forging of my abilities that came through both nature and nurture. My parents doubled down to prove they were good Americans, and deserving of the American Dream. It is this humility, sheer effort, and a focus on education and self-development that shaped my neuro-epigenetic predilections.

I earned my bachelor's degree at University of California, Los Angeles (UCLA) while I was a counselor at the California Youth Authority. I completed a post-graduate Coro Fellowship in LA (see more about Coro on page 28). This enabled me to obtain a Master's degree in urban studies at Occidental College. I finished my MBA at University of Southern California (USC) while I was President of the Southern California Cable TV Association. For 10 years, I hosted a live weekly radio program called *"Asian Understanding"* on the SoCal NPR affiliate KPCC for 10 years.

When I left the media, I embarked on a career in higher education, and was appointed as one of the youngest Vice Chancellors in the University of California system at UCLA. After a decade there, in 1996, I became the founding CEO of *OnlineLearning.net*, a pioneering start-up in online higher education. Our company's systems and processes were merged into Walden University, and I have been on their board for 21 years.

Later, I headed *Big Brothers Big Sisters of Greater LA* and was the first CEO of CK-12, a Silicon Valley start-up. During this time, I was appointed to the prestigious board of the California Community Foundation (CCF) in 2003. Later, I became the Executive Vice President/COO of CCF, and what would later become one of the largest philanthropic grantmaking foundations in the country. We raised more than $2.5 billion and granted more than $2 billion to non-profits around the world. I was privileged to help, advise, and counsel thousands of individuals and families about their philanthropy.

In 1992, I started to lead workshops for executives about managing career and organizational change. That side hustle has taken me all over the world, for 30+ workshops every year. Thousands of leaders have attended, both virtual and in person. These conversations pushed me to start blogging in 2008, resulting in more than 1000 posts. The current iteration, *Your Weekly Ass Kicker,* is going into its 5th year.

I know that is a lot. My asymmetrical career has sculpted my point of view. It has taught me the great benefits of reflection, re-calibration, and re-generation, pushing myself and others to not fall asleep while living, nor fall victim to the prison of conformity and self-domestication.

I am most grateful to be here, in this life, and to have fallen head over heels in love with my wife, a woman I met on a plane 40 years ago. To be the proud father of three college graduates with no student debt. To enjoy the meditative qualities of golf. To resist all the pressure and urges to grow up.

All of this has conspired to help me write this book. The words come from these sources and other origins unknown. It is the

story of my family and my ancestors that energizes these pages
with the hope they might also energize you.

What about Cristina?

For those who doubt the American Dream, I am here to report
that I immigrated to the US in 1999 with two suitcases, a box of
books, and $64 in my pocket, translating that into a grueling but
satisfying ride through business, philanthropy, art, and real
estate investments. Today, I take nothing for granted while
periodically failing to guardrail an ego the size of Texas.

Born in Eastern Europe at a time when being different could
have been a death sentence, I was (ironically) given by the gods
a natural drive to become the best. It is a pointless but relentless
process of preventing dissatisfaction. While I love my life and
what I get to do, the potential glimmering in the distance must
be ravenously and obsessively pursued, and always in high
dosage. Humility, not optional, but always tenuous.

I am the product of communist Romania and the dismal life of
deprivation and disruption that came with that. In such
environments, there are few choices: the oppressors squash
your spirit if not murder you outright, you kill yourself to
escape, or you grit your teeth and find some measure of
purchase on the sheer cliffs of life. After trying some of these
options for size, I turned to writing stories at the age of 10 to
express and process my experiences. I won my first literary
award when I was 17, capturing gold in a national competition
for emerging artists.

Quest is book #16 for me, and I cannot adequately convey how
strong of a lifeline the word we write could be. Please, write
your answers to these questions! It will help you.

I started my first business in high school despite the fact that
having a business was illegal, and then I went on to become a
start-up founder six more times on both sides of the Atlantic. I

have a degree in economics (because I first thought that money is the answer to everything), an MBA (I later thought that maybe business is the answer to everything), a psychology degree (then I realized that getting into people's heads is really where it's at), an executive leadership degree from an Ivy League school (since maybe all our current problems are actually gaps in leadership), and currently I am painfully working my way through a PhD in regeneration and sustainability (that's what the world is asking of me, and obviously, I am somewhat of an intellectual masochist).

I have worked in global corporate environments, philanthropy, and the social sector for more than 30 years, and right now, my professional sweet spot is in building transatlantic strategies at the nexus of the public and private sectors to bridge hardcore economics, neurobiology, and the urgency to improve the human condition.

When not at work, I am consumed by idiotic compulsions to take care of old people, plus urges to understand quantum physics, garden, collect fine art, design/build houses, and explore the world (89 countries and counting).

Beyond my passions and obsessions, I have been reluctantly shaped in my knowledge and psyche by community, by the people I work with, by the values and stubbornness of friends, and by the metaphorical scalpels yielded by those whom I call family: my 3 sets of parents (biological, adoptive, and step–parents), my 8 siblings, my husband, and my children: a daughter, a foster-nephew, and my dog-son who, with divine simplicity, has taught me, that in the end, life is just about love.

Who are the young contributors?

We were well into this book project, when I, John, opened my big mouth and suggested to have the thoughts of youth added to the answers. I said, *"Wouldn't it be amazing to have some unfiltered voices from young people?"* Cristina asked me to say more.

"While you and I have written our erudite insights", I said, tongue-in-cheek, *"as you know, kids do say the darndest things, and their words might just cut through our bullshit and speak truth that could inspire our readers."*

Cristina paused, gathered her thoughts, and declared *"Actually John, I don't think we even have a book without this!"* I immediately regretted what I said, thinking this would delay the project. But Cristina was adamant, which sent us on a journey. It was one of the many moments I have cherished during this process of working together: the challenge of making something worthwhile, constantly polishing it, weaving our two perspectives into something that could truly help people.

We created an interview form for written responses, realizing that would not suffice, and then directly interviewing dozens of young people. We also received audio recordings of friends and relatives talking to grandchildren, and of parents asking their offspring questions, all and all, thousands of answers involving young people from *"I am six and three quarters!"* to *"I am 19 years old"*.

Although tedious at times, the interviews were touching, poignant, and revealing. Most youth provided shorter answers, some elaborated. Despite the fact that older teenagers were more performative than the innocent little ones, we captured some jewels that knocked our socks off, and we are proud to share them with you (protecting of course their identity in the process).

We came away convinced that such a blended conversation with young minds is both useful to their development and profoundly insightful to the adults listening.

Because I, John, cannot leave well enough alone, I then went a step further, and engaged AI services. I generated dozens of demographically diverse profiles to provide hundreds of fascinating responses, some of which are shared here. We believe that the aggregation of AI-generated answers blended with the answers from the flesh-and-blood kids, will fully reflect the zeitgeist of a generation. As you read, we mixed actual youth voices with AI to give you the broadest insight possible without distraction. To transparently acknowledge the AI contributions, we marked them with an asterisk.

All in all, adding the free-spirited and less conflicted words of our youth was an essential and illuminating process.

We hope you agree!

Our charitable recipients

Quest was born out of the connection of two philanthropy executives who dedicated their lives to helping others give back, and the writers encourage readers to find their best and most generous selves. <u>All proceeds from this book will be donated to two nonprofit organizations: Coro Southern California (Coro), and the Daniel K. Inouye National Center for the Preservation of Democracy (Democracy Center)</u>. This is the spirit of *Quest!*

Coro Southern California: founded in 1942, Coro's mission is to strengthen the democratic process by preparing individuals for effective and ethical leadership. Coro operates on the belief that meaningful impact comes from collaboration: people in business and communities, schools and unions, government and nonprofits, working together to find creative solutions and strengthening democracy across all sectors and all political viewpoints. The organization equips people with skills, knowledge, and networks to work together and drive innovative solutions wherever they are.

Coro graduates gain a deeper understanding of how the world works, the leadership skills to improve it, and a network of engaged and influential peers to help them reach their goals. Coro has a unique educational approach that is based on the medical residency model, in which the anatomy of the community replaces the human body. Participants are exposed to multiple, cross-sectoral perspectives, and pushed to see the other side. They are treated to a rigorous experiential process of self-reflection and self-development to expand their outlook on the complexity and interconnectedness we face as a society.

The Daniel K. Inouye National Center for the Preservation of Democracy (Democracy Center): a program of the Japanese American National Museum, the Democracy Center builds on the founding vision of U.S. Senator Daniel K. Inouye, examining issues that seek to divide us, and the shared values and beliefs that unite us. It is a place for education and civic engagement, exploring the rights, freedoms, and fragility of democracy, helping to build bridges and find common ground between people of diverse backgrounds and opinions.

Founded in 2000, the center produces year-round public programs, exhibitions, and educational materials.

———————————

Today, we believe that we need programs like Coro and the Democracy Center more than ever. We hope *Quest* can provide more support to help them grow and sustain their efforts.

Spring

What is Spring?

Beginnings. Hopefulness. Newness.

The promise of it all.

Who am I?

<u>Sam, 17 years old</u>: I am a member of a species that dominates a rock which is floating in space.

<u>Cristina</u>: Ultimately, identity has to be about feeling and thinking - not about what you can see from the outside. I am a soul with a body, having this earthly experience through the gift of aliveness. Born female but queer, I am white in an American context, and not so white when visiting the place I come from, perpetually teetering between ages which are never right for the actual age I find myself being.

I am human. Alive. In love with existence as it filters through my sensory input - colors, scents, sounds, taste, touch, plus everything carved in me by feelings, thoughts, and behaviors. I am the consistent but everchanging nexus at life's intersection, chiseling myself further by the virtue of being here right now.

<u>John</u>: Shapes form and dissolve.

As my life unfolds, I constantly get greater insight into who I am, while not fully certain who I might be. My identity becomes continuously clarified and perpetually blurred, and I open up to the forces that created this form. Within the form is this energy, this essence, this being connected to everything else: "me", yet just a bunch of molecules that dance with other molecules.

I put labels and words on myself to facilitate an ability to move through the world, and I find those words coalesce and dissolve in their relevance. I cannot think too hard about what it all means, but when I step back at a different level and try to describe myself, there is a formlessness, there is a spirit within me that I equally resist and embrace, a spirit that defines and refines how I think about who I believe I am.

And now's your turn: **Who am I**?

What do I want?

<u>Lily, 15 years old</u>: I want to be happy. Isn't that what everyone wants? I imagine life is like a video game with a simple goal: to be happy. And I think that in life there are mini levels, or missions, to get you to happiness. You can't just be happy; you need to do things that make you happy. And so, I want to do those things.

<u>John</u>: We want a lot of things. Some things we definitely don't need, and some things we don't even have an interest in, but we still want them. The words we use have a way of trapping us. They are often robotic and inadequate. Deceptive.

A friend of mine, Akuyoe Graham, taught me this: *"John, when you describe the things that are important to you, you must use the delicious words, the tastiest, the rich and juicy words. When you hear the words, you should understand that those words mean something to you; special. It is important to not be using other people's words, or words that you've heard or read, but words that are as precisely connected to your taste buds."* So, when your boss says, *'what do you want?'* and your wife says *'what do you want?'* and even when you say to yourself: *'what do I want?'* - you need to find the most delicious words possible.

<u>Cristina</u>: Everything. I want everything, because our experience of flesh and time is given so we could practice how to be alive. I want the breadth of community, humanity, love, emotion, as far as it can go, and as deep as possible. At the moment of my death, I want to know that I have pushed to its limits this brief glimpse of light that life is, to its fullest, to its furthest, to its most profound. It's not about the materiality of things. It's about everything between me and the edge of the known unknown. Everything.

And now's your turn: **What do I want?**

What is my purpose?

<u>John</u>: As my ego has exhausted much of its useless energy to self-promote and show that I am better than others, I now simply focus on doing less harm. My little wagon is connected to and dependent on all the other wagons that ever were. I exist to add value to the world around me. My usefulness stems from savoring what is, and thinking of ways to appreciate it. My purpose is asking myself ongoing questions and living a life that is an experiential answer.

Above everything, my purpose is to love unconditionally.

<u>Antonio, 12 years old</u>: My parents and teachers want me to do well and be a good person, but I'm still trying to figure out who I am and what's important to me. Sometimes I wonder if I'm supposed to have it all figured out already, but I guess everyone has to find their own way.

<u>Cristina</u>: I remember the first answer I gave myself decades ago: *"I exist so I could learn, because life is school."* Later on, I said to myself *"I exist to experience existence as a mortal."* Then I said to myself *"I exist to help others and make the world more beautiful."* As a mother, I murmured *"I exist so I could give birth to my daughter."* And now maybe, maybe, perhaps, perhaps, who knows, a different line of thought takes shape: *"I exist because the gods can't do anything by themselves; they need us, humans, to laugh, to dance, to live mortality through us, and do with our hands the mysterious things they deem worth doing. I am a tool for the divine, and a cell in our planetary ecosystem. I might know what my function is, I might not. But I am here, and thus, existence validates itself."*

Ask me in ten years, I'll probably say something different.

And now's your turn: **What is my purpose?**

What is success?

<u>John</u>: This is such a troubling question with a bespoke answer that can be given by only one person: you. The outside world defines success in many different ways, while internally, whatever way we conceive of this definition is a matter of temperament and self-expression.

I look at people that I have admired, famous people, people that have externally achieved almost everything. For example, Robin Williams is someone I always admired. His talent! His amazing influence! His ability to make people think and laugh! Yet internally, he had so many demons which devoured his sense of fulfillment.

What was success to Robin Williams? We'll never know. Fleeting moments of fame and extraordinary genius. He will be remembered for incredible external successes and how he made us laugh and feel. And that he left us too early. He seemed to have everything, and clearly, that wasn't enough.

So, let's remember that nobody can define anyone else's success. You do it for yourself, and I do it for myself.

<u>Milo, 12 years old</u>: Success isn't about being rich or famous. It's about finding what I want and getting that. *

<u>Cristina</u>: Success is many things that shift and morph as we move through life. Layer on this our diverse religions, geography, cultures, the generations we belong to, our gender and values, and the definition of "success" expands so vastly, it becomes difficult to grasp.

In a pinch, we could narrowly define success through two indicators: money and survival. Crass? I know, but also, unambiguous, which all definitions should be.

To get this out of the way, while obviously success doesn't mean just money, money is an easy-to-understand metric. I have friends who have a gold Olympic medal or are on the Forbes list of whatever-whatever, and yet still live with their parents because they can't afford to be on their own. That ain't success. Success without money is just notoriety. True modern success always comes with a financial representation of the energy behind the work. If you meet successful people that have no money, and you believe them to be indeed successful, one of you is confused.

Above all, I think "success" means one single thing: survival. Success is staying in the game long enough to get to a point where existence beats the averages.

Did company A stay in business for 100 years? That survival is success.

People X and Z, were they married for 60 years? The survival of the marriage is the success.

Did startup C sell for a billion dollars? That just meant that as the work was moving forward, it survived yet one more payroll, one more investment round, one more product pivot.

Success is survival.

And now's your turn: **What is success?**

39

What will make me happier?

<u>John</u>: Consider the half-life of happiness: how long does it last? Happiness is one side of a coin. Once it lands, it flips to the other side, which is emptiness or sadness. We are driven by the insatiable thirst for more, but happiness evaporates fast, and I know that the only person that can make me happy is, me. And I feel that happiness always has a shadow: the inquiry into what could have been, a guaranteed pin to pop the happiness balloon.

To be happier, before I exhale into what's next, I must breathe in the "now" and fill my lungs with the oxygen of enjoyment.

<u>Mikey 6 ¾ years old</u>: Giving cuddles and watching a movie with popcorn always makes me happier.

<u>Emery, 17 years old</u>: Ultimately, being happy comes down to this moment. Is this moment good? That is contentment. It is the place where there is nothing more to do. No struggle or battle to fight. I am simply appreciative of what is, I like the way things are, and I would be okay if it were to be this way forever. I am content with this version of reality.

<u>Cristina</u>: "Being happier" is such an horrible concept, I just want to kick it in the crotch. Too much pressure! The need to be "happier" feels like a constant race towards something which is ultimately untenable, because tomorrow I then need to be happier than today, and if I want to live into three-digit birthdays, such a mandate becomes quite the stratospheric lift of expectations.

I think "happy" is enough. Let's take a lesson from the pitfalls of capitalism: less benchmarks please! "Happy" doesn't need constant growth that strips the environment of its raw materials only to taste like sand in the end.

And now's your turn: **What will make me happier?**

What is energizing me?

<u>Judith, 14 years old</u>: A sense of hope and possibility. I am both excited and afraid of the future. I can be energized by the potential to be me and live a fulfilling life, within a supportive community and with friends who accept me for who I am.*

<u>John</u>: Energy is the currency of life. I need it. To have sufficient energy is like a drug. It's not about being high, but about the challenge of being completely present to listen to others, invest in myself, and be fully self-aware.

We each know when our energy tank is low: we can't really muster compassion. We feel anxious. We feel impatient. Even 'hangry'. When our energy is low, our needs supersede everything, and the ego separates us from others. We ruminate, fretting about the past and worrying about the future.

For me, getting energized is a constant effort against stagnation, an effort to get enough rest and eat right. To exercise. To find some tranquility that will allow me to sense this exact moment.

I have to be connected to my breath, to actively be conscious of what I am thinking, and not let heavy thoughts transport me from where I am. Then, when I'm fully present, everything becomes an empowering source of energy: the place, the people, the problem, the pain, and the pleasure.

<u>Evelyn, 13 years old</u>: Sometimes I get random bursts and other times I can't motivate myself to get out of bed. What gives me energy is a mystery.

<u>Cristina</u>: For me, the future is incredibly generative. Dreaming, planning, imagining, are all the equivalent of hooking me up to a juice generator. Looking into the horizon and anticipating the

emerging tomorrow fills me with the nuclear fusion of all that's possible.

When I set my mind on something, I feel currents buzzing through, and my hands start aching to do stuff, build and bring something into being from the nothingness that was there just shortly before. I get giddy, and want to run forward to find the path from where I am, to where I want to be.

"How could this new thing be done?" often becomes the sexiest and most energizing question. The demiurge in me is having a ball, and that becomes the double helix of giving energy while getting energy. What's not to love?

And now's your turn: **What is energizing me?**

What have I always dreamt of doing?

<u>Cristina:</u> If it's a dream, I won't let it go while I still draw breath. When I am tired, I rest - I don't give up. When I am discouraged, I give myself a pep talk - I don't give up. If it's a dream, why give up?

Please don't be one of these lame-ass people who reduce themselves to window-shopping life. If you dream about something, get going. It might take a while, but you'll be heading in that direction. You might not get there, but you will be closer. On occasion, you might even find out that the world wanted that exact thing to happen anyway, and that everything was just waiting for your commitment in order to plop such dream in your lap, seemingly unearned. Rest assured; you deserve it.

How long would it take? What it takes.

How long will you be at it? Until it's done.

<u>Troy, 13 years old</u>: I live in a challenging neighborhood that makes day-to-day living hard for people. I have always dreamt of escaping the life I have. I have always dreamt of a better future. I want to go to college and have a good job. These yearnings seem out of reach at times. I hold onto the hope that I can make the dreams real. *

<u>John</u>: My dreams have evolved over time, especially those dreams of wealth and professional notoriety. I remember wanting to be a stand-up comic because I loved making people laugh.

Childhood dreams morph into grown-up dreams, so in time, my aspirations got more challenging: being a better friend, better spouse, and better parent. I dream of becoming a better human by being more compassionate and generous.

Sometimes, I even think about my regrets as upside-down dreams. Because when you regret things, when you regret not getting things that you really wanted, it feels like missed opportunities. Regrets are aborted dreams, things that might have happened had you had the courage, the gumption, and the will.

Today I dream of being ready for my dreams. Does that make sense? I want to always be ready for those precious moments. I want to be ready to act, to pounce, to take the chance. What I have learned is that while dreaming, a dream may just pass you by. We need to stay sharp!

I don't want regrets. That is part of my dream.

And now's your turn: **What have I always dreamt of doing?**

What makes me laugh?

<u>Avery, age 9</u>: Online videos showing how people can get hurt while doing things they shouldn't. Sorry, but it's funny! *

<u>Cristina</u>: I noticed early in life that I often laughed when nobody was smiling, and didn't feel tickled when people were rolling on the floor. Wiring is what wiring is, and when it comes to humor, our brain's mechanical underpinning is heavily woven through culture, lived experiences, identity, temperament, and… hormones. Yes, we are, unabashedly, chemical machines, my friends.

Laughing is an incredible *"tell"*; it blows the door out of our façade and reveals us for the world to truly see, in a way we can't hide or fake because the faking itself then becomes another transparent level. Fascinating stuff.

Laughing is personal.

<u>John</u>: I laugh to release pain and pleasure. And I put a high premium on real laughter, that laughter from the gut which surprises. Not the polite or phony kind. I'm talking about the unexpected explosion from within.

I laugh when a comedian says something that's so clever, truthful, and searing, that it reveals reality in a way that no other form of conversation could. As I previously mentioned, Robin Williams was, I believe, a genius in this regard, including masterful thoughts carefully crafted, to surprise the unsuspecting audience and subject it to a barrage of ideas that would release pent-up tension, alchemizing it into laughter, all disguised as improvisational comedy.

In one of his live performances, I was petrified by the onslaught and after a certain point, I couldn't laugh anymore. Not because it wasn't funny, but because I was no longer physically capable.

I now laugh at myself as often as possible. I laugh at my many ridiculously dumb and crazy actions, quasi-dangerous or embarrassing, current or past. Things that seemed far worse than they actually were. Some of those were only funny then, and some could only make me laugh now. Most of those are moments of great vulnerability and stupidity, during a time when I could not laugh, make fun of myself, or even tell other people about it. Today I am proud of revealing these moments, and to give myself and others a true moment of laughter is music to my ears.

And now's your turn: **What makes me laugh?**

What are my gifts?

<u>John</u>: If I take a step back and consider the abundance I have been given, it overwhelms me. Yes, gratitude takes flight while the burden of expectations lands. There are un-repayable gifts of freedom, consciousness, the ability to dream, and to consider what I want to be if I ever grow up.

These gifts are not lined up in neat little boxes, waiting to be unwrapped. They're hidden within places that I can't see, within the heart and mind. In my DNA, in my chemistry. They are the result of thousands of years of ancestral lineage, plus nature and nurture doing their incredible dance, creating new and untold gifts within. How and when are they to be opened? One thing is for sure: we will never open all our gifts.

I have been fortunate to stumble upon some fraction of it, things I love to do, things I perform well, things that bring me joy, and things I am very confident about. This makes me wonder, where do they come - from whose lives? And what else might be within me?

Every one of us has an inner factory of miracles, tightly and beautifully wrapped. The totality of our untapped, unknown potential, the genius hidden in the attic of our practicality, all of it ready to be expressed, if only. Let's help each other see our respective talents. The greatest gift is to help another see theirs.

<u>Andrea, 15 years old</u>: I think the way my mind works is a gift I am trying to understand. I think in ways other people don't want to, or can't.

<u>Cristina</u>: I have been given with two hands, and that is both joy, and responsibility: I cannot, absolutely cannot waste what the gods and nature have bestowed.

I have noticed that life is better when I combine those gifts with how I make my living. This makes it is easier, I enjoy it more, and I am better at it than if I chose work disconnected from those gifts. When I stay as close as possible to my mental, physical, intellectual, and emotional endowments everything is smoother, from leisure to household chores, and even the unavoidable hardness of life.

The kicker is accepting that I actually have gifts and once in that zone of acceptance, not to be an ass about it, because gifts are relative. Yes, I might be the smartest in the room every now and then, but often enough, there are others around who are definitely smarter than me.

Many are given beauty, physical strength, speed, a silver tongue. Let's use those good things for good outcomes. Simple, no? Such gifts exist, and therefore gratitude is in order. Picasso said it best *"'The meaning of life is to find your gift. The purpose of life is to give it away."*

Accept, cultivate, strengthen, then give it away. Wash, rinse, repeat.

And now's your turn: **What are my gifts?**

What brings me joy?

<u>Mikey, 6 ¾ years old</u>: When I see my best friends and we hug.

<u>Cristina</u>: Maybe joy is only a still frame in my heart, a moment when I hold my daughter, inhaling the sweaty scent of playground dust. Maybe it's flying above the green pastures of England, driving through lava fields in Scandinavia, or boarding a Zodiac amidst glaciers in the Straits of Magellan while holding my husband's hand.

Joy gets amplified when I stop with the intention to really see it, suffusing it with incredulity at being alive, plus the repeated surprise that I am actually here, feeling what I am feeling and doing what I am doing. It intensifies because I am not just witnessing the moment; I feel the air temperature on my face, the sound in my ears laced with birdsong and music, I taste the things that need tasting. I sense the weight of clothes on the skin, the ground beneath my feet, the thoughts swirling, shaping the moment and being shaped by it. It's all alive, in one's personal maelstrom of existence. Joy is there.

<u>John</u>: Joy is a unique standard deviation away from some gradation of satisfaction. Joy is an oasis of purity. It is an all-in and all-out experience. A beautiful crystal blue pool to submerge yourself in. It is the umami of flavors, the climax of pleasure. Real joy is an elusive thing. It's an eruption.

It's not something to create or even design, you have to be open to it. You can try to anticipate it, and in doing so, could miss it. It may arrive with some notice, or might be entirely unexpected. The more you seek it, the scarcer it becomes. I've learned not to crave it, but to simply keep the door of my heart open so it can stay as long as it wants.

And now's your turn: **What brings me joy?**

55

What did I say I wanted to be when I was 5, 10, 15, and 25 years old?

<u>Cristina</u>: I remember being five years old, planting nasturtium seeds at the edge of my grandmother's flower beds, and even then, thinking them too humble and too orange for my baby ambitions. But nasturtium is all I had, and the modest flower bed was all there was. In life, it's good to take with open arms what is, without thinking too much about the rest.

I know there are people out there that wake up one day and say *"I want to be a ballerina!"* (or a dentist, or whatever) then dedicate every waking moment to the fulfillment of that dream. I admire these people, and if that's you, kudos, because so much time is spent answering the darned question *"what do I want?"*

As a teenager, I wanted to be a fashion designer, and then I promptly went and did it, building an underground couture business for local socialites. But if you would have asked me then if that was living the dream, I would have laughed you out of the room: *"NO!"* Sowing microscopic beads on the velvet draped hips of some bitchy lady didn't feel like fashion, and didn't match the glamorous image I had in my head. Then again, most days do not fit our fantasies, and we seldom understand what we're doing until we are done doing it.

Plant the seeds you have been given and see what comes up.

<u>John</u>: When I was five, I wanted to be a policeman: being a good guy chasing bad guys was very attractive. At 10, I started exploring the idea of becoming a doctor, because curing illnesses seemed magical. I was trying on careers like costumes, without any understanding of what might be required.

Around the time when we went to the moon and President Kennedy was talking about the space program, I started thinking about innovations, and things humans never thought possible before.

In high school, I was mesmerized by the transplantation of a human heart, and studied the pioneering surgeons Christian Barnard of South Africa and Michael DeBakey of Houston. I was fascinated that you could take somebody's heart and put it into another patient. I acquired a super detailed model of the heart, learning the differences between the ventricles and auricles, and how important the heart was. It captured my imagination; I did not want to be an astronaut, but heart transplant surgery was something that I really focused on.

I finished grad school at 25, and by then, the idea of pursuing medicine was a long-forgotten ambition. I became deeply entrenched in what was attractive and in front of me. Of course, I never said to people *"oh, I want to be a businessman in the cable TV industry"*! But that door opened, and I entered, distracted by status, money, and what's achievable, putting childhood dreams through the wringer of reality.

In hindsight, I would not change a thing, because through the cauldron of dream disintegration I learned what I did not want and that I could, indeed, always focus on one human heart: my own.

Instead of open-heart surgery, I just want an open heart to tell me, at every age and stage, who I should be.

And now's your turn: **What did I say I wanted to be when I was 5, 10, 15, and 25 years old?**

What makes me, me?

<u>Cristina</u>: My perfections and imperfections are both the chisel and the polished diamond because without any of it, I wouldn't be me. I might not love everything, but I am everything, perhaps begrudgingly and definitely ungratefully.

The more time passes, the more I love the "me" of "me", with more compassion, more kindness, more self-understanding.

Above all, the combination of my genes and heritage, culture, upbringing, choices, and longitudinal learnings have converged to define what "me" is.

<u>Saundra, 10 years old</u>: I am small and young, but inside I feel as big as a mountain. I'm going to stand tall no matter what challenges come my way. *

<u>John</u>: Isn't this THE question? I'm an extraordinary and mysterious DNA Martini cocktail that sometimes, just sometimes, feels good and tastes good. I have been shaken and stirred. I have had glimpses of my own ingredients and origins. But I'm still searching, always searching for what parts of me are yet to be discovered, to be befriended, to be embraced. To be reminded that I am still evolving and capable of becoming. To cherish what I do well, and to explore my failings.

I need to quench the thirst of the drink I am becoming.

And now's your turn: **What makes me, me?**

What place inspires me?

<u>Tanya, 12 years old</u>: The backyard inspires me. There are so many flowers, and they are all screaming at me *"make art of this! Color! Color!"*

<u>John</u>: I love the smell and the palpable sense of *aloha* when I arrive at the Oahu airport! My wife and I met on an airplane when she was living in Hawaii, and for the longest time, when getting off the plane at the Honolulu airport, I would say *"I just love the smell of the islands"*. We dated across the Pacific for nine months, and I made many trips to Hawaii to court her. The island of Oahu is very special, brimming with great memories of love and anticipation.

When it comes to inspiration, there are also great places in time, because inspiration is also that moment when you connect deeply with someone, when you let your guard down, and they too let their guard down; that hard-to-describe moment when you are communicating in a very authentic way. Time stands still and yet flows, you're really listening, and they're really listening. Words, minds, and hearts intertwine. It's an extraordinary place. It's not a place that you can create or design. It happens because you and the other person are ready to enter that space. That is the nexus my wife and I found decades ago at 30,000 feet in the air - and we have never come down.

<u>Cristina</u>: The alchemical power of place transcends everything. I was in a tiny village in France a few years ago walking through a modern art exhibit, when, the simple fact of casually mentioning to a stranger that I lived in Los Angeles brought to me, like an invading army, a full contingent of the local Who's Who, which started with the local know-it-all and ended with the mayor. I could work for three lifetimes and never amass the glow that

the words *"Los Angeles"* can galvanize in a small room a world away. Place is potent.

If you dream of becoming a Pope, move to Rome. If you want to make it big in a given industry, it helps to be wherever the sun rises from in that field.

While a place ultimately combines with the heavy metals of our own identity creating something thoroughly unique and often fleeting, the place is always bigger than the humans at the center of its ecology.

I am inspired just thinking about it.

And now's your turn: **What place inspires me?**

63

What makes me feel younger?

<u>Cristina</u>: Music and dance, like the ocean, envelop one's body in a physical dimension that addresses both the kinesthetics of the skin, and the inner landscape of memory. It is incredibly powerful. Put a certain song on, and I am instantly 11 years old, by the seaside in Romania, wearing borrowed jeans and a lurex headband, dancing with friends in an impromptu disco under a streetlight, and feeling beautiful. Music is a time machine.

Above all though, I feel young when I go to the edge of what's possible. I feel myself roaring on the inside with power and possibilities, and that's intoxicating. I lose myself in the work, forgetting how old I am. When in that zone, I have no age at all, sublimated as a quantum being of sheer power.

<u>Andrea, 16 years old</u>: I don't want to get old. I like being young. I already wish I was younger.

<u>John:</u> The answer has changed dramatically at different stages of my life. Parts of me are perpetually trying to reach back into youth. The mind doesn't really age much. To feel young is to feel free, to be at play.

Moments of play are the most youthful sources of energy. Floating on calm ocean waters while looking at magnificent clouds. Being silly with young children who are not caught up in the appearance of things. Feeling young and feeling old can converge. There is a dance of perspectives and emotions. This plays out on the pickleball court: I can envision the shot but my knees remind me of what's real. My once cool ideas have suddenly become classic and nostalgic. I have become a blur of young and old. But through play, we can always surrender to joy, and fun itself never gets old.

And now's your turn: **What makes me feel younger?**

What is my untapped potential?

<u>Celia, 16 years old</u>: My untapped potential is the manifestation of what I could achieve despite my disabilities. What I can do that others may not expect of me, simply because I am disabled. I have the great potential to persevere and to overcome obstacles. No matter what. *

<u>John</u>: It's nearly impossible to say what someone could do. We've all heard the stories of what adrenaline and effort can yield. Things that were previously thought to be impossible, have been done.

We can't see potential. We sense it once in a while. There are whispers and clues, things that energize us in ways that can't be described, but we're distracted by the rush of life, often trying to be somebody we're not.

The forces of domestication and conformity are so great, that our potential gets overshadowed by what is marketable. Like a great seed that never gets the light, the water, or the good soil, potential rarely gets a chance. It's crazy. This is what the neuroscientists have found, what the epigeneticists have seen: that we all have unexpressed DNA, that we all have vast caches of neuro-potential that never gets tapped.

Sometimes we have to get help to see our reflection, to be quiet and pause, to listen to what other people are saying, and to consider what our heart is whispering, allowing those magical seeds to sprout, grow, and seek light.

<u>Cristina</u>: My intention is to die as old as possible, as close to my potential, and in any which way, but not in my sleep. I want to die staring death in the face, experiencing it fully, knowing that every second leading up to that finite point was completely squeezed of the juices of what is possible.

Life is about life; about playing existence as the violin that it is, as deeply, as loud, as long as possible, and for all it could be played. The quest for potential can be nothing but a love letter to life, and a pledge of everlasting service to it. I hunger for this, probably always will, and fear I will never reach it.

I love the being of "being" so much, I am scared of not doing justice to the magnificence of what life gives us - the gifts, the mission, the potential itself that we are here to embody, and by embodying it, thus serve.

Potential is very counterintuitive. We think we reach it by deploying discipline, while in reality it looks as if it's destiny, happenstance, luck, and freedom that bring us the closest to our fullness. That journey is woven through a paradoxical process of building a safe space for our souls, a space of exploration, passion, randomness, convergence, something that gets continuously triggered and revealed. In allowing this to happen, we align the groundwork for confidence in who one is, and who one could be.

Potential is service. Potential is applying all that we received from the gods, until the moment our gifts get used up and the tools break. Potential is, in equal measure, an exciting door and a heavy burden.

I might never find out how far I can push it, but I can nevertheless commit to going to the limits of myself and everything around me every second of my life. Because why not? My supreme fear, for myself and for everyone else, is not living enough while living.

And now's your turn: **What is my untapped potential?**

What is one way I can make the world more beautiful?

<u>Emery, 17 years old</u>: Fully expressing myself helps make the world beautiful. Beauty comes from a certain genius, a certain pattern of thought that is sculpted, written as words into a story, drawn on paper, or painted on canvas. If I did more of that, then I could be more authentic and generate beauty. I would also help my community and spread whatever beauty I can.

<u>John</u>: I always thought that I had something to contribute to make the world better and more beautiful. But to improve something, you must know it, yes? There is arrogance in this mindset.

As my eyes open, my mind and heart sense more, and I realize how beautiful, expansive, extraordinary, and unknowable the world is. Not only the spectacular flora and fauna in the extraordinary magic of mother nature, but people, and the human environment I have the privilege to occupy. The depth and breadth of its beauty is something that I rarely appreciated in the past, because I looked for specifically beautiful things instead of seeing the beauty that's already there.

How naïve I have been to think that I could make the world beautiful! There is beauty already in everything and everyone. Nowadays I simply hope that I can open my apertures wide enough to take in as much of the beauty that envelops me.

<u>Tanya, 12 years old</u>: I do my art, share my art, then show people how to do art. To have the world become more beautiful, it is good to be kind to people. If someone looks sad, maybe give them a smile, maybe give them a hug... Ask what's wrong; if they don't want to tell you, well, then they don't want to tell you. But you tried to make the world and their day, more beautiful.

<u>Zachary, 16 years old:</u> The world can be more beautiful when there is less stress. I want to help people deal with their stress so they can enjoy life. This would be beautiful!

<u>Cristina</u>: I am obsessed with the idea that my life's mission might actually be to make the world a more beautiful place.

I have committed to live every day in service of this potential mission. By doing so, my life becomes beautiful, and the lives of all those touched in the process become more beautiful too, because we are wired to respond to it. Beauty is an irresistible sun: everything in its orbit experiences a gravitational pull.

This combination of our world + a human life + transformative action influencing others towards their own, more beautiful universe, equals something that is worth the discipline, the effort, and the commitment.

Please, choose beauty! If we are going to use a napkin, choose a beautiful one. If we are going to serve someone food, let's put it beautifully on a plate, no matter how humble. We choose things all the time, every day; so why not choose only beautiful things? A beautiful city, a beautiful song, a beautiful dish, a beautiful thought. Not because beauty is shallow and pleasing to the eye, but because beauty is the external manifestation of evolutionary progress.

And now's your turn: **What is one way I can make the world more beautiful?**

When do I feel connected to the universe?

<u>Thalia, 12 years old</u>: My connection with the universe happens when I am by myself, when I have the time to think about what has happened in my day, or what's going to unfold with the people around me. I connect with the universe when I am walking my dogs, because I am alone and I think about the world, about myself, and my family.

<u>Mikey, 6 ¾ years old</u>: I feel connected to the universe when I am happy and when I feel I'm big and strong.

<u>John</u>: I feel connected to the universe when the ocean is at my feet, with the sounds of the world only as waves and water. I look at the clouds and I am transported as my little, infinitesimal life, becomes hyper-clear.

I feel connected to the universe when I'm at the edge of a mountain and all I see is an extraordinary web of ecosystems that are alive without any acknowledgement of what I'm doing. I'm just another microorganism, doing whatever until I die, and then ready to be returned to the earth. Paradoxically, that smallness I experience in such moments makes me feel connected to the vastness of the collective ocean, and part of it.

I feel connected to the universe when I meditate and let go of the trappings of a modern world, as I deeply sink into a quiet, peaceful world of darkness, suddenly a soundless, and almost senseless being, floating, a tiny creature moving between other tiny creatures in an endless space.

<u>Cristina</u>: Connection comes at random times, but mostly in nature.

Connection comes at random times, but mostly in the presence of beauty.

Connection comes at random times, but mostly when rested.

Connection comes at random times, but often when loving and filled with appreciation for something presented to me by the gods.

Connection is sacred.

And now's your turn: **When do I feel connected to the universe?**

What gives me pleasure?

<u>Andres, 13 years old</u>: I just love that feeling when people think I am doing a good job. That's when I'm truly happy. *

<u>John</u>: Because we are in a perpetual search for pleasure, expectations often ruin everything, and anticipation undermines the destination. Real moments of pleasure emerge unsuspectingly.

When I happen upon a sunset, a flower garden, a piece of art that is enormously powerful and it captures my imagination, the body transports me to something special. I feel good; I feel connected.

I get pleasure when the solution to a long-standing problem emerges from seemingly thin air. I get pleasure when I'm sitting in a movie theater, and my wife holds my hand for no particular reason. I get pleasure from hearing the sound of real laughter!

Pleasure is a surprise, not a strategy.

<u>Cristina</u>: I am by choice an Epicurean in the Ancient Greek way, and by birth both a Taurus, and a Romanian; a one-three-punch perpetually pushing me to hedonism.

Pleasure is a decision, an intentional experience with a source that changes all the time, on a spectrum from birdsong to touching my child's face. If it is to pick the #1 thing that gives me pleasure beyond the obvious things like food, sex and awe-inspiring landscapes, I would pick the feeling of being the best.

There, I said it.

Being the best (at anything) is both need and want. I am honestly a bit terrified of the day when I will stop being the best at the myriad aspects of my existence - and if I am lucky to live long enough, that day is surely coming.

In the meantime, I intend to be the best for as long as possible, at as many things as possible, because that gives me pleasure beyond measure.

And now's your turn: **What gives me pleasure?**

What is a good life?

<u>Thalia, 12 years old</u>: A life is a good life as long as you can take care of yourself, and others can take care of you while you take care of them.

<u>Emery, 17 years old</u>: Ultimately, a good life has a balance between doing good for as many people as possible, while also having time to actually enjoy each day and have fun. A good life is having an emotional home that I can return to when this monstrosity of a goal is pulling away my life force. A place I can go to regenerate, so afterwards I can go back to my ambition. It would be good to have both.

<u>John</u>: I've come to realize that a good life is a life that is infused with my values. A good life is by definition subjective, defined by who I am, how I treat others, whether I cared about others as much as I cared about myself. A good life is the courageous life lived fully and authentically, not the life others expected that I lived. A good life is a life that, however brief, helps others live good lives too.

<u>Cristina</u>: A good life is a life lived in love with oneself.

A good life is a life where, at the end of the day, you're squeezed like a lemon because of all the living, learning, and feeling you've done. A life immersed fully in the nuanced complexity of existence - loving, helping, exploring as much and as far as possible, both inside and outside one's self. A good life is a life where the next step is guided by what the world needs, a mandate for one's soul - however hard that might be to follow.

A good life is being a good friend, a good offspring, a good sibling and grandchild to someone, a good spouse, a good parent, a good employee and employer, a good citizen.

A good life is not wasting time, not wasting the strengths and chances we were given, while feeling grateful for it all. Some humbleness and some boldness are always part of a good life. Lots of laughter, mistakes, dead ends, wrong turns, moments of shame and anger - that too. Some degree of connection with nature; that's a must. Kindness also, without a doubt.

And despite the fact that each individual's good life will look and feel different from any other good lives lived out there, two things will always be part of what makes a life "good": a significant amount of zest for something (anything), and leaving the place better than found. That's it.

And now's your turn: **What is a good life?**

What is on my Bucket List?

<u>Cristina</u>: Decades ago, way before the commercial space industry was a glimmer in Richard Branson's eye, I learned that one can go to the edge of space even if not an astronaut - all you needed was cash and courage, which granted, is a key set of ingredients in most things.

That piece of intel exponentially expanded the sense of possibilities my mind was willing to entertain. Such expansion, in conjunction with the inherent power of a simple list, can be transformative. I know that if I would have put *"go to the edge of space"* on a piece of paper that day, I would have been there by now. But I didn't, so I haven't. Yet.

We, humans, are easily distracted. The years pass by, and we find ourselves on our deathbeds still far from all that is glorious and wanted, simply because we are periodically detoured.

A Bucket List is under our control. It is not about privilege, it simply makes things concrete and specific, enabling us to understand the destinations we want to pursue. If I didn't have a Bucket List today, I would make its development my absolute priority because it would provide not just a North Star, but a whole constellation of stars, all pointing North. That's powerful.

<u>Joey, 8 years old</u>: Buckets? Lots of buckets. *

<u>John</u>: I think a Bucket List is an appalling symbol of privilege. *"What things can I do that are somewhat out of reach, or beyond my ability to purchase?" "What are the things I crave? The experiences that make me feel special?"*

Everybody has dreams; the size, dimension and the contents of one's bucket vary remarkably. Those with less, think of the most ordinary of needs; and those with a lot, think of extraordinary wants.

I remember compiling such a list driven by the desire to impress others. While I always included something I truly wanted, the list was a symbol of my ambition and imagination, all designed to make me look good. Over time I found my lists to be superficial, a mere vehicle to improve my status with others.

Don't get me wrong, I have a loose list of places and experiences I want to enjoy with others. I still seek mind bending conversations. I want to fully sense things that give me energy and humility, but there's a change from "my" bucket list of "me" things and "I" adventures, towards something deeper.

It's not that I'm wisely settling into the boundaries of my purchasing power. It is not about having a bucket of small, sour, and egotistical grapes.

I want my bucket to overflow with love, compassion, hope, and as much authenticity as possible. I do not need to travel to the far reaches of my emotional landscape, in order to visit the edge of my capabilities to be generous, compassionate, or loving.

Because of this, I am excited, and my "new" Bucket List is richer, seemingly infinite, and absolutely affordable.

And now's your turn: **What is on my Bucket List?**

Summer

What is Summer?

Warmth. Progress. Time.

Growing up to meet the opportunity.

Where do I come from?

<u>John:</u>

Stardust.

I am from the beginning of time and the end of the earth

I am from the 50's and a December birth

I am from Tomiko and Yoshimi

I am from rice and sashimi

I am from an accountant and an artist

I am from the fields of Cienega and Salinas

I am from San Jose and LA

I am from yesterday and today

I am from my children and my wife

I am from a socially conscious life

I am from an immigrant's hope and an American dream

I am from okazu and green tea ice cream

I am from a yellow face and an Asian race

I am from boulder creeks and oak tree forts

I am from running track and basketball courts

I am from the Issei, the Nisei, and the Sansei

I am from mentoring, luck, and generosity

I am from farming root and urban wing

I am from nothing and from everything

<u>Tanya, 12 years old</u>: I come from a lot of places, almost everywhere. My DNA chart is very complex, so it is hard to list it all because I am so mixed. The main ones are Mexico, South East Asia, and Romania, but there is much more. My soul is coming from existence – I don't know if that's an actual place or not, but I think I come from that place that makes things exist.

<u>Cristina</u>: I come from the same plane of existence where I will be going after the death of the body. Mysterious, and yet, simple. We arrive here, from somewhere, and then we leave, somewhere, and the nature of our life seems to solidly but never categorically point to the rather obvious answer that "here" is just a brief stop, an experience that our souls have, for a little time.

I come from where I am going.

I trust deeply in this.

And now's your turn: **Where do I come from?**

Do I trust myself?

<u>Cristina:</u> Absolutely.

Yet, paradoxically, I am reminded, time and again, that I cannot completely rely on my own human perception. And I am fine with that unreliability.

I have been in crowds seeing things which, upon reflection, couldn't have been there. I have overlooked truths that were screaming at me with a Boeing 787 roar. I have missed cues the size of elephants. I have suffered from purposeful, self-induced amnesia erasing large swaths of behaviors and activities out of my head for no other reasons than the redundancy was unnecessary.

The brain is funny. That thing the brain does to help us process the information we receive, the mental chunking, the data discarding, the inferences, it has a price which we pay daily and happily so we could function and not be paralyzed.

So yes, I trust myself, absolutely, but not fully. Does that make sense?

<u>Sofia, 16 years old</u>: Human emotions are complex. How can I feel such deep love and empathy, but also be capable of cruelty and hatred? Understanding my heart is a never-ending puzzle. *

<u>John</u>: As I'm getting older and less tolerant of ambiguity, I feel like I'm trusting myself a little bit more. Is it expediency, or is it experience?

Nonetheless, I am filled with habits woven into my neurons, and these habits sometimes confuse me and take me back to the beginning of a process, which, most of the time, I actually do not want to restart. Humans are creatures of habit. We find ourselves in the middle of a cycle which seems like *déjà vu*, only to say *"This always happens to me. I always do things like this. I will never do this again."* But we do.

Not trusting myself is really about not understanding myself. To consciously trust the self, I have to be awake and present.

And now's your turn: **Do I trust myself?**

What sacrifices have past generations made in order for me to be here?

<u>Thalia, 12 years old:</u> The list could go on. My dad, who is originally from Peru, came to America for a better education, which gave me a chance in life. Also, my teachers continuously sacrifice, work hard, and do whatever they can to help.

<u>Cristina:</u> EVERYTHING! It would be safe to say that past generations have sacrificed it all for me to be here.

My paternal grandmother confessed that in another life, she wouldn't have married, craved no children, and would have danced her life away sunbathing in green meadows while wearing pretty dresses. Which is not what she did! Between backbreaking work that literally broke her back, the hollowed womb that birthed seven kids, and the savagely bruised flesh bestowed upon by violent domesticity, she gave us all she had. And that's counting nothing in the ledgers of history, or harvesting the sacrifices of bone and soul of other ancestors, unknown or known.

To simplify, I'll call it all a tax on comfort: they sacrificed what could have been, not for a guarantee of my day's bounty, but for a chance at such, today. They gave it all because there wasn't any other way; an offering. Thus, I am here.

From such a vantage point, all things they sacrificed are boons, indubitably. But the true gift comes from looking at myself through their old eyes: what I never have to suffer, the power I hold, the staggering array of choices they couldn't even dream, but of which I can still find it in me to complain on occasion - all of it, a form of future sacrifice they didn't know they made.

I did not ask them to endure the woes they did, and can't alleviate the pain they felt so long ago; but I, in turn, could vow to see today's fine beauty and live its richness fully. That, I do owe.

<u>John</u>: I am Japanese-American.

As I look back at the silence of those who sacrificed themselves so I can be here, and the things they had to swallow to survive, I feel the weight.

I am tested by trying to help my own kids understand the sacrifice of their predecessors. My namesake grandfather, John Toraichi left the land of his ancestors as a teenager with no possessions, worked hard, built a life in a new land, and buried four of his children before he was 50. As I mentioned in my bio, my great-grandparents were obliterated in the Hiroshima atomic explosion. My grandparents, parents, and all of my uncles and aunts, endured baseless incarceration during WWII. It is impossible to describe these sacrifices. They are ungraspable. And yet, my kids are fundamentally removed from this collection of sacrifices.

There is a great silence between the facts and the stories, and so many tears and broken dreams, scattered between courage and quiet endurance. All I can do is create the space for my children to do what their grandparents could not do.

There's always residual, historical sacrifice that is different for every generation. My father's generation aimed for something tangible: *"We are going to prove ourselves, in dignity and silence, and turn out as the best. We won't talk about it; we'll just go and do it"*. A different ethos.

Our aim was to assimilate and fit in, holding a focus on not making trouble, intent on being "successful in America." In contrast, my kids are constructing their identities very differently and, in my eyes, equally beautifully.

We have traced our family tree for 36 generations, back to the 12th century. When you do such ancestry work, you realize that most things are never written, and that even what was known was not shared, because that's not what people did back then. More silence.

The brick at the base of humanity's story is the thread of leaving something behind never to be regained again. There would be no "now" without whatever they created "then". Even if we don't know exactly what they did for 36 generations, we can imagine, and in honoring it, we honor ourselves and our children.

And now's your turn: **What sacrifices have past generations made for me to be here?**

How am I misunderstood?

<u>Andrea, 16 years old</u>: I think a lot of people make assumptions about how I present myself. But I know there is a lot more to know that's not on the outside.

<u>Cristina</u>: Being misunderstood would be a step up. I personally feel that most of the time I am down-right invisible. Being misunderstood would imply that someone took the time to actually see me and decode (however erroneously) my essence. But nobody cares, my friend. Nobody cares. Being misunderstood is a privilege.

If anyone understands even an iota, we should cherish that. And because of this, let's speak up about our needs, let's cultivate whatever level of empathy suits our worldview, and then expect nothing in return.

<u>John</u>: Misunderstanding starts when we're trying to be something we're not, which for most of us is all of the time. Our faces, our hearts, our words, and our actions are often not aligned.

My need to be respected, acknowledged, and liked overwhelms the authenticity of the exchange. Yes, we are misunderstood because some people are uncaring and dismissive. But mostly, I am misunderstood because I have failed in making my interests and ideas clearly known. I think the greatest misunderstanding about me has been what I have not understood about myself.

And now's your turn: **How am I misunderstood?**

What gives me pause?

<u>Luca, 15 years old</u>: The suspicion that I might be doing something wrong always gives me pause. There is a whisper in the back of my head asking me to take a beat, and I listen to it.

<u>Cristina</u>: Everything gives me pause. Everything.

Everything has, tucked inside, meaning, learning, joy or usefulness. All that is, and all that happens, is another way to experience the world, if we could only pause and notice.

<u>John</u>: Real eye contact. An amazing sunrise. A giant redwood. A eulogy. A laughing child. Mesmerizing art.

I am addicted to the moments of existence when a pause really stops me in my tracks. When a pause makes me think, wonder where I am, and ponder where I'm going. When time stands still, and I start to see, hear, and feel differently from the way I did just a moment before.

I believe that such a pause is not a function of our inner remote control, or some gap between the words. This kind of pause is intent made manifest. It is a decision to stop reacting, a decision to breathe and notice, to be quiet and still, feeling my heartbeat. This is the brief infinite space when mind is acute and attuned to what is truly happening

There would be no music without the room between the notes— the pauses.

It makes me wonder about the nature of life. What if life is, actually, just a long pause briefly interrupted by our living?

And now's your turn: **What gives me pause?**

What is my relationship with nature and living things?

<u>Mikey, 6 ¾ years old:</u> When I am outside, I connect to trees and the garden, and they give me their breath. I breathe the trees in, and when the wind blows, we all breathe together.

<u>John</u>: It's strange how disconnected we can become from the natural world, living solely in our little minds, thinking our little thoughts, and believing ourselves completely separate from other living things.

Because my urban existence makes nature a foreign place that I visit as a tourist, I have to reorient and reconnect with what's real. This periodic awakening from my cosmopolitan delusion reminds me that I am just a small molecule in the incredible fabric of nature.

I need a regular refresher to drive home the point that I am of this world and still in it, that where I begin and end, and where nature begins and ends is impossible to discern. That we all need each other: my oxygen, the air's nitrogen, the plants' nutrients, and the earth's minerals. That I am neither the chicken nor the egg.

When I walk amongst the trees, snorkel in the ocean, or look into the heavens, I can be jolted back to my tiny status on this not-tiny planet. In that awareness of my own minute scale, I melt into the atomic structure around me, knowing that I impact and am being impacted by everything. Knowing that my actual degree of control and free will are extraordinarily limited. And I find a paradoxical sense of deep agency, not in the abandonment of my own sense of being, but by surrendering, I become part of everything.

Andrea, 16 years old: I love nature. I always try to be in it. I also love my phone. I try very hard to put my devices down because I know I need to sit and just be with nature.

Cristina: Objectively, my relationship with nature and living things is the same as the relationship between my right eye and my left eye. There is no separation between me and nature, despite what I have been told, brought up to believe, and repeatedly conditioned. We don't even need to discuss it.

Subjectively, I absolutely love nature and living things, especially plants. I have always loved plants, and worshiped forests, mountains, and the sea. I never get to spend as much time in nature as I want, but any moment I can, I cherish. Nature is everything!

And now's your turn: **What is my relationship with nature and living things?**

What answers am I looking for?

<u>Emery, 17 years old</u>: I would like to know what purpose is in one's life. When I find this answer, it'll allow me to rise up and step on that platform, spending time defining such a purpose, then living it.

I would additionally like to understand what really fills my soul and makes me happy.

I'm also very confused. I keep wanting to make decisions now for my later self. Having these answers would be exactly what I need so I can move forward in a way that allows me to feel good about the choices I am making.

<u>Cristina:</u> Not to be too circular about this, the answers I am hunting are almost always the same: how am I doing in relation to what I need to be doing? What do I want in relation to what I seem to be choosing? Do those I love, love me? What does the world need from me?

The recurrent, often daily feedback is deeply necessary, even when uncomfortable. But *"this is the way"*, Mandalorian-style.

<u>John:</u> Like every good student I've been trying to get good grades, do well in school, and understand things in an above-average way.

I was hoping that there would be beautifully engraved answers and crystal-clear solutions to the problems of life. Ironically, outside of the field of mathematics, the answers are constantly evolving. Life is not a quadratic equation; it's not a scientific measuring process. It is a hypothesis that begs experimentation which seldom leads to finding out the answers, but at least it clarifies the hypothesis.

All I can do is broaden the premise, while simultaneously narrowing the scope, and maybe that path leads to a more precise answer. This is, however, the inverse of what the life formula for the questions of existence requires.

This quandary has pushed and pulled me to seek, if not better answers, then better questions.

And now's your turn: **What answers am I looking for?**

What is beauty?

<u>Cristina</u>: Beauty is the cocaine of my existence, the foundation of any and every one of my pursuits, from words, to landscapes, art, buildings, work, babies, puppies, clothing, one's household and, well, everything.

Beauty is leverage and war. Desire. Metric. Evolutionary trick. Beauty is evolution. Beauty is our future. Beauty is the whole thing. Absolutely the whole shebang.

I believe we have the choice to make all things beautiful - from laws to a sandwich. From friendships to garbage trucks, professional interactions, paper bags, pens, and milk bottles.

We should make everything beautiful. And because we can, we must.

<u>Sofia, 16 years old:</u> True beauty is a reflection of the soul. *

<u>John</u>: We are awash in education about what looks good, what is attractive, what is sexy, what is beautiful. Our minds have been domesticated by layers of socialization, advertising, media, and biased by the dominant culture, nationalism, and ethnocentricity. As such, beauty has been carved out of the ambiguity of our minds by commercial enterprises, and we are thoroughly indoctrinated as to what a face should look like. What a body should look like.

"Beauty is in the eye of the beholder" is both true and trite because the beholder has been carjacked and is currently controlled by a mindset that views beauty as a capitalist commodity. It is important that we fight our way out of conformity and the subliminal, intentional pressures to define what is beautiful. This is a full-time job.

Once the commercial scales slough off our eyes, we can reclaim our capacity to see what is truly beautiful, and give back its useful lens to our individual inner eye. Only then can we use the power to push back on what is force-fed to us, getting back into the driver seat of the infinite expanse of beauty.

And now's your turn: **What is beauty?**

What expectation of me, that others have, interferes with my success?

<u>Tyler, 12 years old:</u> I think it is hard for me to be successful when people underestimate me, and don't see what makes me unique. Anyone who puts me in a box, by definition, will limit who I am and what I can be.

<u>John</u>: As the oldest of four children, I always felt there were greater expectations of me than the others. Being first is challenging. Yet, those expectations, real or imagined, helped shape my identity. As we grow up, we accumulate expectations that are layered atop those occurring from within. We truly can't discern the full origins of how we came to expect certain things of ourselves, or why we think others expect things from us. Expectations can bulldoze over life's uncertainty and smooth out the road ahead. Expectations can also be mirages that can never be reached regardless of effort. We spend a lifetime fighting, digesting, and adopting expectations.

Ultimately, we each have to decide who we want to be, filtering, fighting off, or befriending this tyranny. Bronnie Ware's study of hospice patients yielded their biggest deathbed regret: *"I wish I'd had the courage to live a life that was true to myself, and not the life others expected of me."*

<u>Zachary, 16 years old:</u> I have friends who are afraid to try new things, which forces me to fit in and do what they want and not what I want.

<u>Cristina</u>: I have put other people's expectations at the top of my own list systematically, which is never a good idea, and most definitely quite a gut-punch for one's self-esteem. In the end, if what others expect and what we expect from ourselves doesn't match, it will never work.

People will perpetually try to mold us in their own image, or at a minimum, will try to get us to sign their manifesto for life (or work, or marriage, or "being a man" or "being a good mother" or whatever). Ultimately, if it doesn't fit, it can't last. If it's not "me" I'll never be particularly good at it, so while I could listen to what others are saying, in the end, I have to discover my own truth, and my own set of expectations. That's plenty.

And now's your turn: **What expectation of me, that others have, interferes with my success?**

What is my relationship with money?

<u>Aaron, 16 years old:</u> As a young artist, I try to remember that money is not everything. True success and meaning often comes just from what I create and what I am passionate about. Money is necessary but is not what will define me. *

<u>Evelyn, 13 years old:</u> I know that when I think of money, there is a part of my brain that sees something different, something cute and pretty. And it's easy not to think about the money when I really want that something. So, I try to ask myself: "is it useful, this cute and pretty thing?" Usually, it isn't.

<u>Cristina</u>: Money is oxygen. Money is electricity. I like and need both oxygen, and electricity. While oxygen, electricity, and money can be hurtful in a given context, ultimately, they have no inherent morals and it rankles me when people disavow money. I don't get it! You don't need oxygen?

When it comes to money, I respect its power and I understand its four separate forms (how to make it, how to use it, how to save it, and how to multiply it), which are dramatically different from one another. I also understand that money is simply a tool, just like electricity. And I know that I need it in vital ways for the existence of everything and everyone I hold dear, just like oxygen.

I know that money is ultimately just a joint language for day-to-day living - because who wants to ferry goats to the market in exchange for potatoes or what-not? Waving a piece of plastic is exponentially less cumbersome.

Maybe I have such a clean relationship with money because I never had any back-up. It was very clear that if ever in a jam, there will be nobody coming to the rescue.

I was like an astronaut living on an otherwise abandoned space station, with only a tinfoil wall between oneself and the merciless deathly void, you start looking at oxygen and electricity in a new way. And then you see the sun, out there, infinite everything if only you could learn to harness it. So, you do.

When it comes to money, the most important piece is to disentangle "money-as-a-tool" from the emotions, values, dogma, prejudice, trauma, fear, and marketing of "money-as-a-manipulation-medium". It is essential to learn how money works, and it's not that hard. Once that understanding happens, freedom comes.

John: I have a love/hate relationship with money, and it's very dysfunctional.

We all need money. We all know that we want money. How much money do we really need? There is never enough.

There's a psychotic power that money can have over us when our wants extend far beyond our needs and means. Money becomes emotional. We can blame it on the capitalistic industrial complex, we can blame it on the way advertising is targeted and personalized, building an insatiable desire to consume, buy, and collect material things - but we are ultimately responsible.

When I was younger, I never reflected on these thoughts, I just conformed and dove headfirst into the river of materialism. Over time, I have fought my way back to the surface and on to the safety of the shore to analyze my attachments.

When money is in control, particularly in the form of debt hanging over one's head like the darkest cloud, it is hard to be authentic. When we have very little of it, we dream of having much more. When we have a lot of it, we still dream of having much more. We start to realize the addiction, the psychological control it has on our life. How it defines our literal and figurative self-worth.

When I was growing up and working hard, I wanted to impress people with things, with experiences, with the symbols of success. It was important for me to have a particular type of car, or a particular type of watch. I believed these symbols would galvanize respect from others. I wanted to broadcast to the rich: *"I'm like you"* even though I was taking a fake elevator to the penthouse.

I never negotiated a salary. I did not take jobs for the money. I was a very bad financial advocate for myself. Despite all that, I was always surprised at how much my compensation was, and was equally surprised at what things cost and how challenging it was for my family to make ends meet in non-luxurious ways. To support my family and to pursue lives and careers that were less materially oriented, I had my hustles, and during the roughest of times, I had the help of friends and family who got us through.

I have reconciled my relationship with money. To want what I have, to want less, to try and minimize my wants over needs. To not compare myself to others.

I wish I had learned these lessons earlier. Now in control, I like money.

And now's your turn: **What is my relationship with money?**

What is my need for prestige?

<u>John</u>: Prestige is the champagne sibling of "status" and the caviar cousin of "respect". This pseudo-family trio is driven by ego, by the need to be held in higher regard. To be liked and adored. To be better than others. I have lived with this trio all my life, wanting secretly to get much larger doses. Being famous was part of my definition of success. I have received awards and recognition, more than I ever imagined and certainly deserved. I want to believe that I have earned these moments, but if we pay attention, there is always an ulterior motive.

I craved the prestige, the status, the recognition because in the Western world, we are suckled and suckered on the ersatz of competition and meritocracy. But the need for prestige also stems from weakness and craving respect, plus the fundamentals of human nature: to feel distinctive and acknowledged, while leaving a mark of semi-immortality in this world: *"I mattered!"*

It is easy to think that fame or visibility equates to goodness and perhaps greatness, or that it validates a life well lived. And yet, we know in our hearts that if fame is a goal, our life will have to bend and contort toward bright lights that cast a dark shadow.

The goal of prestige is a great distraction from living true to one's potential.

<u>Cristina</u>: The need for prestige is like "the Force" in the Star Wars universe. Use it one way, and it can make you a hero. Use it another way, it can make you a villain. Both equally seductive, but thoroughly divergent destinations.

Let's not question the existence of the need itself. We might or might not succeed in excising the sin, and even if we do, what guarantees are there that the terminus point would be any loftier? None, really.

Let's take the shortcut, and use the need for prestige as fuel, because ultimately, it really doesn't matter to other people what is motivating my good deeds. Let's make the need yield to the goals, let's wall it behind a values system, and then just ride the wild horse of "prestige" to a more virtuous home.

And now's your turn: **What is my need for prestige?**

What is my plan to become a better human?

<u>Lily, 15 years old</u>: I'm trying to be less judgmental. I want to not have biases about people before I know enough about them. And I want to have more of an open mind. Like: *"I won't try cauliflower because I think it's disgusting"*. I've never eaten cauliflower. I want to change that mindset, try new things, be less closed minded, and less judgmental.

<u>Emery, 17 years old</u>: I want to gain more perspective. Talk with people and mix their ideas with my own. A lot of information is hidden because we're wearing lenses that are tinted for a certain color. We are blind to the many colors that are there. There's a lot hiding in plain sight. When I seek more perspectives and get more lenses, I get a bigger picture, instead of just seeing the same things over and over again on my own.

<u>John</u>: All change begins within.

There's no operator's manual for life, so we listen to our parents and watch other people, trying to figure it out. At some point, we think we know who we are. But what are our failings and foibles? I don't mean we have to always be strengthening skills and competencies, becoming a better accountant, improving our golf game, or being a better public speaker. I'm talking about our humanity, our ability to love, to have compassion, and to be generous.

I've asked this question many times in interviews - our HR departments never liked it because it seemed too open-ended, but I was just curious to see if the candidate had a plan. A high-ranking official who wanted to join my team gave me an adequate answer. Six months after we hired her, she stopped me in the hallway and said *"I want you to know I have not had a good night's sleep for the last six months because of that question. I knew it was an important question. I want your help and I want this organization's help in making me a better human."* And she laid out an extraordinary roadmap about how she needed to improve her humanity. We looked at each other and I said *"I'm all in."*

<u>Mikey, 6 ¾ years old</u>: My plan to become a better human is about being kind and helping people that need help.

<u>Andrea, 16 years old</u>: I have to be better to myself. To be a better human being I have to understand myself more. The better I understand who I am, the better I can be.

<u>Cristina:</u> Perhaps all that we need is to remember that we are born perfect, each and every one of us. And to respect that initial perfection, that pristine humanity that might still be there, at the center of the heart.

I aspire to hold the space for people, so they too could allow that next-gen humanity to surface, and then we might jointly hold our kindness as a vessel for who we each truly are.

On a day-to-day basis, I am in a constant pursuit of that cranked-up betterment because there is no stasis. Others will kick us off our chairs in the labor market, the flesh will sag, inflation will hit our accounts, the things we thought as truth will be proved erroneous. But it is easy to run the hamster wheel of becoming a better human, so balance is called for here.

To be a better human, I need to get myself to first believe that everyone else is actually a better human than I might judge them to be.

And now's your turn: **What is my plan to become a better human being?**

Can I give my all without ever knowing if it'll make a difference?

<u>Lily, 15 years old</u>: You might not have confirmation that it will make a difference, but you don't have confirmation that it won't. So why not try? If you don't give it your all, what else is there? You might as well.

<u>John</u>: I want to live in a world where we each consciously add to the great work that has preceded us. I believe that in the end, our work is to nurture the seeds, to plant the trees that will generate the fruit, the shade, and the timber, to make a difference for a world of beings we will never meet.

If I want to make a difference, and be given the credit for it, building my legacy, that's a very specific kind of *"making a difference"*. When I am truly compassionate, truly generous, truly creative, when I am giving my all, wholehearted, without ego, I trust that such an effort is enabling the best outcomes, the biggest impact, and the most profound difference I could make in the world.

This does not mean that we shouldn't plan. We must. We plan, then we give our all.

And we accept that the seed never sees its flower.

<u>Tanya, 12 years old</u>: You never know for sure if what you do will make a difference, but if I am pretty confident about it, I am going to try to give my all, and if it doesn't work, it doesn't work.

<u>Cristina</u>: We can take the small crumbs of significance that are given to us on occasion, but let's not stop to wait for it, and let's not feel discouraged if the recognition doesn't come. Nothing is what we think anyway; nothing is what it seems, nothing feels

the way we expect it to feel - we are poorly calibrated for our own, media-honed expectations.

The older I get, I split the doing from the knowing, and take the meager water droplets disguised as feedback, then move on. On and on and on.

Give it all because death will take all anyway, so why die with a full tank?

And now's your turn: **Can I give my all without ever knowing if it'll make a difference?**

How accurate is my moral compass?

<u>Lily, 15 years old</u>: Most people probably say that their moral compass is accurate. Our perception is that everything we believe is correct, and everything that we think is good, which cannot be really true.

<u>Cristina</u>: I do not think that we could even know the answer to this. What might we even use to calibrate that compass? Is it the Bible? Buddha's teachings? The Torah? The Quran? The law of the land?

Sigh.

Maybe just asking oneself the question is the point. Maybe searching for such a magnetic pole is more important than finding it. When in need of alignment, I personally try to keep True North at *"kindness"* although it swings wildly through the cardinal points of *"anger"* and *"ego"*. Like with any compass, building the practice of dialing that metallic face-plate by hand again and again is incredibly artificial; but it works.

<u>John</u>: Recently, I took my moral compass to the shop because it stopped working. I thought it was broken or that I needed some parts, maybe the batteries were dead.

There was a long line of impatient clients at the customer service counter of *Moral Compass Emporium*. It was fascinating to overhear all of the problems people were having. "Out of warranty", "Needs software update", "Made in Russia".

When it was my turn, the moral compass engineer told me that my particular compass should have had an expiration date. That my version, which was top of the line when I was born, was obsolete and unreliable. While some basic rights and wrongs have not changed, he told me that much of what was once right is not only wrong today, but shameful. The new model was open source. It was plugged into the latest facts and research, and had filters for political correctness and social media bias. The software is auto-updated. Still requiring manual settings and personalized calibration—meaning I still have to think.

I finally bought the new one. The engineer warned me as I left: *"We all have to be careful; what is right today could be an embarrassment tomorrow."*

And now's your turn: **How accurate is my moral compass?**

Where does my self-doubt come from?

<u>Lily, 15 years old:</u> When you get a bad grade in school, you definitely feel self-doubt. You're like, *"oh, I failed this math test. I'm not smart"*. Which is inaccurate. Just because you're bad at taking tests doesn't necessarily mean you're not a smart person. Parents, teachers, and authority figures will make you feel like you're not enough, by their standards. But you still have a place in the world. If you remember that there are people that won't make you doubt yourself because of whatever happened, then you'll win.

<u>Cristina:</u> Eh… Who cares?

Doubt is how the gods test us. Doubt is like the weather, and self-doubt is just a deeply personalized weather system.

Maybe grandma's voice is ringing loudly in our narratives. Maybe trauma is kicking vigorously. Maybe social media is triggering things. Maybe what is being attempted has never been done. The bottom line is this: sometimes doubt will cycle through our hearts twice in a twenty-minute interval. Other times, we won't feel it for years. Either way, the unpredictable bastard has only the teeth that we are willing to give it.

Just keep going.

<u>John:</u> Self-doubt and its origins are exotic and diverse. We all have it. The question is not whether doubt will exist in our hearts, but whether self-doubt will be the primary challenge to becoming who we want to be. Doubt will be continuously generated in the ventricles of our hearts from birth to death, as one of the irrelevant fluids that is coursing through us. It does not give life, and it need not be fatal.

Like a weed in the garden, it is a great de-traction and dis-traction that sucks the life out of the soil of what is real and important. When we give it our mindshare, self-doubt takes over the spaces that should be flourishing. Self-doubt is a shadow that is always present. It lurks.

When we ignore it, we are stronger.

And now's your turn: **Where does my self-doubt come from?**

What would give my life more meaning?

<u>Evelyn, 13 years old</u>: Finding my passion! I hope that in the future I will be able to find something that makes me want to wake up every day and say, *"Okay, I want to do this!"*

<u>Cristina</u>: Jackie Robinson said *"A life is not important except in the impact it has on other lives."* That's it.

That is the one and only thing that I am interested in, the one and only dimension I am investing my energy in, during every remaining moment of the rest of my life. This is why I write; this is why I build; this is why I work, the only significance worth pursuing with voracious hunger and atomic energy. I get jazzed up just thinking about it.

<u>John</u>: If we are honest and stop to think about who we are, what we are doing, and what is vital, we realize that we are in an infinite ocean of meaningfulness.

Meaning surrounds us.

I am not talking about things that are meaningful on the path to impress, nor things that fulfill societal expectations. We could get so caught up in the shininess, the brand, the "what do other people think" mentality. Strip all that away because this is about our souls.

We can't shop for meaning. Ultimately, the source of it, how it's defined, its dimensions, how to get more of it, has been there all along, inside of us, part of us. The search for meaning is a search inside ourselves.

And now's your turn: **What would give my life more meaning?**

Why don't I get the credit I deserve?

<u>Kenzi, age 11</u>: Because I don't ask for it.

<u>John</u>: The Zen archer focuses on their own skill, knowledge, and ability; not on the target. Sadly, very few of us are Zen archers.

While we legitimately are deserving of respect, we know that money or prestige guarantee nothing. Are we here to win? Or is there a larger purpose? In the end, the shelf to store our awards is only as wide as our real pursuit of the good, and most credit comes at a cost.

If part of our goal is to seek such credit, it will undermine the work because it alters how we make decisions, how we engage in relationships, build, and communicate. The need for credit takes effort and energy away from what we could achieve. I believe that if we're doing what we love, and if we're doing it for a purpose greater than ourselves, the credit will follow. Once we make the decision that we should get more credit than other people, we destroy the potential of our deeds.

I simply want to forget that! I just strive to become a great Zen archer and simply pull back the bow.

<u>Cristina</u>: 99% of the time, I do not allow myself to think about credit. I don't even allow myself to feel something in relation to credit because, by design, my work is invisible and impossible to detangle from other people's. The more invisible it is, the better I am doing my job.

Yes, every now and then, the imbalance hits hard, and I buckle under the cumulative chafing mentioned above. I get angry. Really angry. I get voices in my head saying *what's the point of doing any of this?* inflating my righteousness like the hot-air balloon that it is.

And then, do you know what I do? Absolutely nothing.

I let the pain flow through me and move on. And let me tell you, it is not just *"pain"*, it is a tsunami of ego and aggregate soul-bruising, plus a raging storm wrapped together with the kind of suffering that even Putin might not deserve. Yet, I let the pain flow through and then move on.

I know that it will always be back. Not sure when, not sure why, but it will hit me again and again.

If any adjustments to my course are required, I make them gratefully because gift-wrapped in the pain, there are always insights. And then I keep going, because you cannot do the social impact work that I do while worrying on a daily basis about getting your due. In the ashes of that purifying pain I always find diamonds, and when this happens, the ersatz of something unnamed dissolves into something else, also unnamed, but better.

The Fates test us in funny ways.

And now's your turn: **Why don't I get the credit I deserve?**

Why do I feel that I am not enough?

<u>Sam, 17 years old</u>: Comparing myself to others will always make me feel that I am not enough; that I am not being as good as my peers. The comparison gives me a lot of self-doubt when I see somebody else succeeding at something that I am attempting.

<u>John</u>: In nature and in life we always live contradictory experiences rife with emotions that ebb and flow. We have confidence, and then we have a lack of confidence. We feel sufficient, and then we feel insufficient. We are courageous, and then we are cowards.

Doubt, fear, and inadequacy are always ready to fill the space that is briefly occupied by our most positive conceptions of self.

If we're brutally honest, we're always in the transformative trajectory of becoming something more, something different, something closer to what we were always meant to become. Beyond the exponential growth of our brain in childhood and the long arc of that plasticity, our consciousness continues to grow even as our body declines, so maybe feeling incomplete is a normal state.

So much of what we are and what we could be has been pushed down beneath the surface, derided, mocked, ignored, and marginalized. Our potential, that sense of what we want to be, the soulful urges to express, are blunted, not by malice, but by conformity.

We talk of diversity and individuality, but we don't like it when things stick out; we are uncomfortable when things are different, so we've developed our own process of suppressing ourselves. Sometimes we don't even know exactly why, and it just aches inside, an ache which requires us to listen, to find solitude, to awaken to our own internal voice, and most importantly, to stifle all misgivings, at least temporarily.

And if we are still, and if we can bring ourselves to eavesdrop to our heart, then and only then, we will find the path to becoming who we were destined to be. To feel enough for a time.

Yet, it can never be enough. We need to find a way to live with that.

<u>Cristina</u>: Excuse me, what is the KPI of *"enough"* please? Asking for a friend.

I am a woman. I am an immigrant. I might or might not be white. I have a Latino last name in America, a country who loves to have their lettuce picked by lettuce-picking Mexicans, and also a country which would rather have only neighborhoods from where said Mexicans depart every night for the other side of the proverbial border fence. I am a former starving Romanian child from a society rooted in second-class citizenry, communist slavery, and an absolute lack of human rights. Pick any of the above, and you will find a media narrative explaining why I should feel that I am never enough. But I'm alive, therefore I am enough. The light always wins if given a chance. Survival is proof that I have been enough at each turn.

Whatever your journey, you too are alive and are here today. This is all you need to know beyond reasonable doubt that you are, and have always been, enough.

And now's your turn: **Why do I feel that I am not enough?**

What role does luck play in my life?

<u>Tanya, 12 years old</u>: Luck is everything! Luck is why I have decent parents, my talents, and great friends. Luck is all.

<u>Sam, 17 years old</u>: Sometimes I feel lucky. Sometimes I think things happened by coincidence. Other times, I think things happen because I'm making them happen. There's always a reason. I don't think luck plays a big role.

<u>John</u>: What's luck got to do with it? (Sounds like a very strange rendition of a Tina Turner favorite; sorry/not sorry!)

Luck is a function of being in the present spot because of an infinite set of circumstances that preceded this spot. This is way beyond control or comprehension. Is that luck?

My grandfather survived the 1906 earthquake in San Francisco. Was that luck?

My mother was born as the 10th child and survived, while her four oldest siblings died before she was 15. Luck?

My father was enlisted into the military, but was not sent to war because of an injury to his arm. Lucky?

All we experience is a result of the random and inexplicable turns that life produces. Is that luck? Or is that life?

Luck has nothing to do with anything, and also, luck has everything to do with everything. We don't pick our parents, birthplace or genetic material that determines so much later on. Most definitely we didn't pick our ancestors and the entire millennia that preceded us to form our culture, preferences, and ideas. We did not pick the subtle and unknowable things that shaped how we see the world and why I prefer mango ice cream over peach sorbet.

I think I'm lucky because decades ago I happened to sit on a plane next to a woman that stole my heart and became my life's partner. I think I'm lucky because I have three healthy kids. I think I'm lucky because I was able to retire with enough resources to last for the rest of our lives. But the truth is that such thoughts are nothing but feelings of good fortune for which I have gratitude. My true luck, where forces beyond my control came together, is what made me, me. All the component parts, built, constructed, and ultimately manifested from a magical, mysterious, and unknowable realm.

Did I work hard? Did I pay attention? Did I try the best I could? Yes, yes, yes, I believe so. And yet, that has nothing to do with the foundation I was given by sheer luck. Everything I ever did, all efforts, each intention, the sum of my actions reside upon, and depend on, the great, random, and ancient bedrock of chance.

<u>Cristina</u>: Luck is both everything and nothing.

Luck is everything because a person's specific probability of being born is about one in 400 trillion. Also, luck is nothing because responsibility, thankfulness, and positive events seem to be empirically correlated. The more intentional I am about my choices, the luckier I seem to become. Everything is luck, and nothing is luck.

And now's your turn: **What role does luck play in my life?**

How much longer shall I wait?

<u>Lily, 15 years old</u>: We should never wait for something to happen. When we want something, or when we need something we simply just have to make a change.

<u>John</u>: There's power in being patient, in watching things progress, seeing what actually happens, and not trying to anticipate. It is essential to periodically wait, to stay in the moment, listening to what someone says before concocting our response. Deferring gratification and being patient is good in this context, allowing what's going to happen, to actually happen; that's virtuous.

I work on being more patient. It's never been a strength. I always want people to get to the point. I want people to move, and I am biased towards action. As the saying goes, I'd rather seek forgiveness than permission. It's the way I've been raised and it's in my DNA. I know this, so I'm practicing and always trying to wait more. Not easy! But at least, I can now see the benefit of letting things evolve without my input.

Most of life will occur majestically without my help anyway.

<u>Cristina</u>: Waiting is a mindset, a concept in one's head. So please, never wait. For anything.

Patience? Yes.

Waiting? Never!

Let's enjoy life *"as-is"*. Let's immerse ourselves in the experience of being alive and do the things we want to do. All of it is going to change anyway, so why *"wait"*?

Even if, let's theorize, you are a pregnant female *"waiting"* 40 weeks for the baby to come full term, you still don't have to *"wait".* Savor the weeks before the birth of the child; be who you are, feel what you feel.

As Rumi says, *"what's meant for us will always find us".* And if not, then it won't. In the meantime, let's spend the time we are given towards becoming that for which that thing we want could happen; let's walk towards it while it walks towards us.

Waiting is wretched, agonizing, pointless. Let's just live patiently, but never wait for anything.

And now's your turn: **How much longer shall I wait?**

145

What is true love?

<u>Tanya, 12 years old:</u> True love is when you are willing to be anything for that person, whether a sibling, a companion, a friend, or a lover. You don't usually know if it's true love; if you guess right, you guess right. If you don't guess right, you don't guess right, but eventually, you will guess right.

<u>Mikey, 6 ¾ years old</u>: Two people who see each other, in their eyes.

<u>Cristina:</u> I think we can only know true love in hindsight. Too many things feel like it without actually coming in two parsecs of proximity to *"true love"*. And I don't care if we speak of people, cats, shoes, pistachio ice cream, or a favorite song - only time tells if that thing belongs to the minuscule box labeled *"true love"*.

My recommendation? Feel it, check in with oneself six months later (or next Saturday), and if you still feel it, it might be.

In the meantime, let's revel in the joy of the thing, the swelling of the heart, the excitations, the vibration, the idiotic smiles, the little dance - imaginary or concrete - originating from this thing, which might or might not be true love. Especially because we periodically use the words *"true love"* and the hearts of those who love us truly, as a substitute for toilet paper. The human heart is a sadistic bastard with masochistic tendencies. Let's just enjoy the ride.

<u>John</u>: When I was younger, *"true love"* was something romantic, perhaps a soulmate. I dreamed of someone special for me, a person that I would love. It was the glass slipper we hand to a special someone to try on, so we could assess their potential by a lofty standard.

It took me a while to learn that true love was not a *"someone"*, but the depth and breadth of the actual emotion. Yes, the emotion can be associated with a human form, but for me, *"true love"* is a test of my capacity to love unconditionally. That love is precious. Not a currency or a spectrum; true love, pure and infinite.

True love cannot be stopped. And the truest of love is all-encompassing. It is not reserved for someone or something special. It is an energy that can be released onto all people and things.

Love on that scale has the ability to mete out justice, to reconcile, and to forgive. It is the centrifugal force, the gravitational pull, the oxygen, which holds us together. True love is the acceptance that we are all inextricably connected.

And now's your turn: **What is true love?**

Why do I care about what others think?

<u>Mikey, 6 ¾ years old:</u> I do not do that!

<u>Cristina:</u> I try very hard not to care about what others think, and I fail every single time, because I have been conditioned to care. If I take just the amount of image management that I do in a given year, I could probably use that to learn a foreign language. From scratch.

It's ridiculous.

For millennia, we depended on the community for survival, and having others' approval seemed to increase our individual and collective odds. The cycle reinforces itself. Conformism is rewarded, divergence is not.

I care about what others think because at some primal level, it holds death at bay.

<u>John:</u> We all think too much about what other people think of us. We adjust our words, our appearances, and our actions to please others, and that can easily take us off the path of who we are and what we want. When other people are thoughtful and compassionate, what they think and say can be useful because sometimes we can't see the truth until the reflection is given to us by someone else. Truth-telling sessions that are kind but digestible, with hard edges delivered in ways that can be absorbed, have real value.

We just have to be on the lookout for thoughtful and mindful moments that help us become the best possible version of ourselves.

And now's your turn: **Why do I care about what others think?**

What good do others see in me that I don't?

<u>Tanya, 12 years old</u>: I see myself as pretty great so far, and most people seem to see me the same way, so probably nothing yet. It is interesting to wonder about this though.

<u>Luca, 15 years old</u>: I don't think I am kind. At least, I don't think I am as kind as people think I am. I don't talk to everyone; Kindness is being nice even if you don't want to. There is a difference between kind and polite; kind is about moral action. While I am kind sometimes, it is not universal in my life. And without that universality I don't feel that I can truly say that I am kind.

<u>John</u>: It's incredibly hard to see myself. Not in the mirror. In the mind's eye, where we perpetually idealize who we see, always younger, more attractive, more on top of it. It's not that we're lying to ourselves; this illusion is how we survive.

I hope people see someone who's trying. Someone who does care; someone who uses sarcasm to defend the vulnerable parts of my soft underbelly. Someone who's really making an effort to find that balance between trying to be real, and being real.

<u>Cristina</u>: We need to trust that our life matters to other humans. To trust that people we might not even know are positively impacted by what we do. To trust that our existence on earth has an effect, however invisible. We seldom know what it is; we just have to keep going, understanding that our life matters.

This impact is like an island in the mist: we don't have to see it to know it is there. The fog might dissipate, we might get glimpses of it on occasion, but even if we don't, it is enough to know it exists. Let's keep going. It's good.

And now's your turn: **What good do others see in me that I don't?**

When do I lose the sense of time?

<u>Thalia, 12 years old:</u> I lose the sense of time when I am performing on stage. Normally, I am not that good with time, I will admit it; I can't really tell if it's been 10 minutes or an hour, but I am really into musical theater, and I belong to a really great community playhouse with a lot of lovely people. We work together, and I enjoy that tremendously, which makes me lose the sense of time.

<u>Cristina</u>: I lose the sense of time when I read. When I dream. When I garden. When I drive long distances - all of it and each of it are rare opportunities to discard my worries and just be.

I think conceptual time is profoundly incompatible with full immersion in our human existence. Sometimes we find our most genuine form of ourselves, and the switch toggles: we could either focus on time, or we could focus on simply being. It's one or the other.

<u>John</u>: Being in flow just happens. The more you want it, the more you won't have it. That is the magic of losing oneself in the activity, in the behavior, in the fullness of the moment.

It happens when I meditate, when I daydream, when I'm between tasks. When I've forgotten what I was doing because of a blissful digression propelling me head first into a rabbit hole of oblivion. I lose the sense of time when my mind has a singularity of unconditional commitment to an idea, a person, an experience. It doesn't happen often. And once it does, if we can understand how powerful, how energizing that moment is, it will give us strong and indelible clues about who we are, what we want, and why we're here.

And now's your turn: **When do I lose the sense of time?**

Could I be generous without expectations?

<u>Lily, 15 years old</u>: It's very hard.

I think I can, but I need to work on myself to be able to do that. To be generous, is too often expecting credit for it. And even if no one is watching, and even if no one else is going to give you credit, it makes you feel better about yourself, which is kind of an expectation. If I do something generous, say, I give money to a homeless person, I do it because I know I'm gonna feel good afterwards.

I think it's impossible to have no expectations, because if you're gonna feel good afterwards, and you know that you're gonna feel good afterwards, that's the expectation. So, I don't know if it's actually possible.

<u>John</u>: True generosity is just the act of giving. It's not about ROI. Not about mutual obligation or *quid pro quos*. It's not even a win-win situation. We're talking about just being generous.

A while ago I met with a philanthropist who wanted to create generosity without expectations, giving gifts to people in need without any paperwork. Today this initiative is called the *Pass It Along Fund*. Someone in need would apply, and they would receive up to $5,000 within 72 hours. There would be no "thank you" letters, no report about the impact, no bureaucracy. The recipient would just have to commit to do two acts of kindness, unsolicited and self-determined. No verifications.

The fund has been going on for many, many years. Tens of thousands of acts of kindness have been generated and undocumented because when we are generous without expectations, it triggers an infinite chain of generosity. So yes, it is possible.

<u>Cristina</u>: It depends. Some of the time, yes, I give freely and without expecting anything in return. Other times, probably not.

The trick here is not the expectation in the moment; it is the expectation removed from the moment. To expect nothing in return while in the moment is easy; but to look back and expect nothing in return while weighing my generosity in the rearview mirror is a more difficult task. Maybe somewhere, deep down, my aggregate generosity gives me the sense of being entitled to rights that are reserved for perpetually generous people. Now, overcoming THAT, is the next frontier for my philosophy.

And now's your turn: **Could I be generous without expectations?**

What does "being busy" mean to me?

<u>Thalia, 12 years old</u>: Being busy doesn't mean doing a lot of things at the same time. *"Busy"* is more about an eventful day with lots of things one after another, like a list that is too long and burdens us. It is a pressure.

<u>John</u>: For 35 years I banned the *"busy"* word. I called it "the B word". You could not say *"busy"* in my presence. Think about this for a second. Listen, for when the word *"busy"* is used. We say it and hear it often, gratuitously.

Everyone is busy. Three-year-olds are busy. Busy is gravity. Busy is a given. It's everywhere. It's everybody. It is also a bizarre status symbol and a competitive sport.

But what are we busy doing? And how is our busyness contributing to our advancement as humans? The word *"busy"* has become an addiction. We value activity over actualization. Let's stop using *"busy"* so we might get connected with everything and each other.

<u>Cristina</u>: I am a strong believer that none of the things we WANT to do will ever make us feel busy. *"Busy"* only exists on the chore continuum.

As long as we are busy, we don't have to do things we don't know how to do, we don't have to figure out what we are on this planet for, or confront the additional 30 lbs. of fat on our ass, the marriage that creaks, and the things we wanted to do as kids and never even came close to doing.

"Busy" is an honorable hidey-hole in which to live a respectable, albeit thoroughly unremarkable and potentially mediocre life. As John said above, *"busy"* is a very dirty word, possibly the dirtiest.

And now's your turn: **What does "being busy" mean to me?**

What is God to me?

<u>Sam, 17 years old</u>: God is something that brings us all together, and that is beautiful.

<u>Cristina:</u> God is a dialogue partner. An amused parent. An absent overseer. A part of me, of which, I am, in turn, a part. Everything is divine form, and you and I are divine form, which means that you and I are, actually, God.

<u>Natalie, 12 years old</u>: Everything. God created everything. God has a plan for everything.

<u>John</u>: I always hoped there was a god, a being that was watching out for us, for me. But I know that's not true. Today I believe that God is a source of energy, doing what it does, without any regard for us, without any regard for me.

God is what explains the unexplainable, all the questions that we can't answer. I know I'm part of that energy, not just some tourist to the world of lifecycles and evolutionary patterns that have been going on for billions of years, and will continue to go on for billions more.

God is within me, in my given talents and in all the untapped, unexpressed possibilities layered within. I know that my atomic structure is part of the atomic structure of all things, and that form of God is a nonjudgmental, non-emotional source that propels us forward through and after life.

And now's your turn: **What is God to me?**

Is there a difference between doing good and being good?

<u>Thalia, 12 years old:</u> These are two very different things. If you are *"doing good"* it means that you are doing something specific, and that something you are doing is good. *"Being good"* is more about being morally good. I like to assume that everyone is a good person inside.

<u>Cristina:</u> Yes, there is a difference, although the distinction matters perhaps only for the person reflecting upon it. For everyone external, all that's visible and relevant is the behavior. And at any length, the *"doing"* can always redeem the *"being"* if redemption is wanted. I think doing good has transformative powers. I don't care if your day job is to shine a dictators' shoes; I mean I care, but I am willing to give you a chance, if, in your free time, you build houses for the homeless and clean plastic from the ocean.

<u>John:</u> When I was naïve and young, I did not understand the difference. Good deeds meant good intentions, yes? Does it really matter what motivated the doers of good? Isn't *"good"* just *"good"*?

I have come to learn that if recognition, prestige, status, tax deductions, barter for favors, etc. are the primary motivators, then the behavior is not fully about being *"good"*. Being good should not be performative; if it is, then goodness is compromised. The ends don't justify the means. Doing and being are one and the same only when, without personal benefit, we do the thing we know in our hearts is good. Yes, it is a high standard. Yes, it is uncommon. And yes, it is worth achieving. Being good is an unswerving, uninterrupted commitment to goodness.

And now's your turn: **Is there a difference between doing good and being good?**

What must I teach others?

<u>John</u>: I have had the privilege to stand beneath the statue of David and be stunned into silence by the 16-foot masterpiece that Michelangelo carved from a single piece of marble.

The artist wrote about his creation: *"I had only to hew away the rough walls that imprison the lovely apparition"*. Michelangelo must have been smiling when he wrote this: yes, just remove the pieces of marble that weren't David, and there he is, freed from his rocky cage!

It makes me think of what weighty stones might have been attached to each of us. The rough pieces that we have accepted and that hide our true selves, obscuring our own inner "lovely apparition". Like Michelangelo's work, unearthing who we are may, indeed, take a hammer and a chisel.

If I could teach one thing, it would be to inspire others to hew away the facets of their façade, the attributes of acceptance, the exterior of expectations, all of which imprisons their souls yearning to be free.

 If I could teach one thing, it would be to know thyself and be thyself.

<u>Aidan, 18 years old</u>: Patience. It is a massive thing that a lot of people don't bring into their lives enough, myself included. When something big goes wrong, and afterwards a bunch of little things start going wrong, and I soon reach a boiling point and explode in anger, I should just stop and think about it: *"Damn, that just happened!"* There's no chance I could have predicted that series of events, and yes, it sucks.

Let's take it easy. Let's let it simmer down. Most things are really not that big of a deal.

This applies to absolutely everyone. Everyone needs to put patience into practice.

<u>Cristina:</u> I must teach others everything I know. Everything.

I am here on this earth to be a conduit of knowledge so our society can go on, and people could have better lives. What I know should go forward, and not be lost. It's a duty, a responsibility, a joy. I must teach others everything I know, plus how to learn about those many things I don't know.

And now's your turn: **What must I teach others?**

What must it be like to be my adversary?

<u>John</u>: I'm not the fiercest of competitors. I can see where compromise makes more sense; where *"splitting the pot"* is better than *"the winner takes all"*, and I think my adversaries can sense that. Perhaps I don't have the killer instinct. Crushing my opponents is not in my DNA.

Don't get me wrong. I want to win. And I play to win. But what is winning?

I remember when I voted for my opponent when I ran for office in high school. I lost by one vote: mine. I still think my opponent was a better candidate than me.

It makes no sense for one person to get everything and for others to get nothing, even if that winner is me. I don't say this because I'm generous, charitable, or equitable. For me, to take it all, or even just more than my fair share, is not logical. This is not something which I have within me.

<u>Cristina</u>: Terrifying. It must be terrifying to be my adversary, if I am being honest.

One has to know what one is.

We are all given missions in this world. I, for example, am a born protector, and as far as protectors go, an arsenal of skills, tools, and sharp weapons is to be expected, together with the willingness to put them to immediate and effective use.

Then again, there is that saying that a master practitioner never needs to fight once they are truly a master. I think that's something to aim for.

And now's your turn: **What must it be like to be my adversary?**

How can gratitude change my life?

<u>Thalia, 12 years old</u>: When I feel grateful, I can help other people feel grateful. If we treat others how we want to be treated, it feels a certain way. If I realize that I am grateful because something good occurred, then I am going to try to make that happen for other people.

<u>John</u>: Gratitude will change the way we view everything. When we are truly grateful for how we got here, what we have, the things that we've been blessed with, it is an overwhelmingly positive frame of mind.

Nothing we have and nothing we are could have been done without the extraordinary, often unknown, and perpetually incomprehensible history that has preceded us. There is a Japanese word that describes this: *"ohn"*, which loosely translated means *"un-repayable debt"*.

There are things we thank people for. And other things that warm our hearts. But we have to remind ourselves of the unknowable and un-repayable debts we have in our Darwinian lineage, and in the world around us.

<u>Cristina</u>: Gratitude is like an atomic bomb detonating in the darkest recesses of the human soul. The more we use it, the less dark those spaces become. Gratitude is, by an order of magnitude, the most effective way I accidentally used to overhaul my existence. The moment I started to focus on it, I was incapable of feeling envy, hate, most fears, and the broadest and often most mundane set of frustrations known to humankind.

Gratitude makes us impermeable to daily annoyances, it makes us waterproof to drama, and prevents the expenditure of gargantuan amounts of energy and time on things that do not truly require it. I would dare say that it might even improve one's health.

This is not theory; this is practice. Try it. Let's try the high-octane fuel for life that grace is, and let's use gratitude as the refinery where you can produce it wholesale.

Once we all adopt the gratitude policy, nothing is a big deal anymore. Life becomes bliss.

And now's your turn: **How can gratitude change my life?**

Am I trustworthy?

<u>Luca, 15 years old</u>: Yes, I think I am trustworthy. If someone wants to tell me a secret, I will never tell it further. I keep my word. That is the simplicity of trust.

<u>Cristina</u>: Yes, but not because of virtue. Because of a perpetually-renewing decision to be trustworthy.

In the society where I grew up, everything was jointly owned by everyone. Hence, nobody owned anything, and stealing was never on the list of the seven sins. In my community, adults honored each other's stealing acts, when, in different circumstances, this would send god-fearing humans running to the confessional.

When you grow up like I did, being trustworthy is a daily decision, a habit you build, one by one by one by one, every day of your life.

<u>John</u>: I do feel a sacred obligation to others who entrust to me their love, and their expectations. I want to be worthy of their trust. I am always prepared to be trusted.

Every moment is a test.

And now's your turn: **Am I trustworthy?**

What gives me peace?

<u>John</u>: Inner peace is being present and centered with a sense of control that lowers stress, a space and time when our minds are clear, confident and non-anxious. This is a great source of personal internal energy supplementing the energy we get from food, rest, and our breath. Authenticity, compassion, and real connection are also associated with inner peace.

I try to be more self-aware, to notice thoughts and emotions rather than just being driven by them, to minimize the turbulence of what others think, and my overly analytical thoughts about pleasing others. That brings me peace.

Inner peace does not come from doubling down on effort; it emerges from the stillness of reflection. Stop. Breathe. Notice. Reflect. Then, respond. To prevent our lizard brains from constantly reacting, we need time, even if just a few seconds plus the air in our lungs. Peace comes with the realization that everything is interdependent. That we are not alone. That little can be achieved by ourselves. Once we embrace this interconnection, we can soothe the noise that comes from trying to do everything alone. For lasting inner peace, we are needed and we need others.

<u>Emily, 11 years old:</u> Sometimes when I'm outside by myself, I feel like everything makes sense, and I don't have to worry about anything. *

<u>Cristina</u>: Besides churches, proverbial banyan trees under which to sit like the Buddha, and wide-open vistas, inner peace is a decision. I experience peace because I decide to eliminate everything that is not peaceful in my heart, mind, and house. Peace is a value, an attitude, an asset. I won't say that it is worth everything, but almost everything.

And now's your turn: **What gives me peace?**

What form of selfishness have I been practicing?

<u>Jayden, 9 years old</u>: I am embarrassed to say this. I do not like sharing my toys!

<u>Cristina</u>: We are all many kinds of selfish, and the line between selfishness, self-care, and the pursuit of one's personal truth can quickly get blurry, especially when examined from multiple perspectives.

As a woman I am actually working really hard to discard the shackles of what has been handed down to me generationally as *"selfish"* because the list of what's considered selfish for a woman is much longer than for a dude. This is not a theoretical argument, or an *au courant* dig on patriarchy, but a lived-to-the bone reality.

I remember last year finishing an 8-hour workday in front of a conference call screen on a back-breaking stiff chair in a hotel room on the other side of the world, and feeling skewered in two by the guilt of being far from my husband and kid, while also knowing that a man wouldn't have thought twice about it.

Gender roles die hard.

A gynecologist told me once to be more selfish in bed: *"your selfishness and your partner's selfishness could create something wonderful."* That was a great piece of advice because once expanded to realms beyond sex, it can really fuel the magic of a fabulous relationship. Yes, let's make room for what we each need while our partner makes room for what they need. Nobody can articulate needs better than the human feeling it. At the intersection of our individual fulfillment, the sky will hold room for each of us separately and both of us together.

Why would I feel selfish for putting a human (myself) at the center of my own design? It's called *"Human Centered Design"* because the human is supposed to be at the center of it. Let's rethink what is selfish with kindness and generosity running through, and we'll all be fine.

<u>John</u>: I've been trying to practice a kind of selfishness that is conscious of itself - which is a beast to be tamed, ravenous and insatiable.

This awareness has taught me that I do need rejuvenation, joy, and self-care. I have to find the time to refuel the tank, which in turn, makes me less selfish. I need more than just rest or fun. I need time to restore my engines - through exercise, golf, and meditation. I need alone time to forget my thoughts and my to-do list. I want time to learn about the needs of others. Time to regain perspective.

This is a knockdown, drag out, wrestling match to quiet the beast of selfishness. And in those non-self-absorbed moments, the animal naps, and I regain some parts of the self I need to be.

And now's your turn: **What form of selfishness have I been practicing?**

What habit must I build?

<u>John</u>: I am working on reducing the time that elapses between my authentic thoughts and the expression of those authentic thoughts. Particularly practicing the loving and compassionate transmission of my constructive thoughts.

I am working on my ability to navigate awkward moments and transcending the habit of hesitation, getting myself to not succumb so easily to a phony smile and a nod, plus a set of empty words to avoid that instance. I am working on fighting the thought that *"this might not be the right time"*. I am working on seeing and addressing the great resistance and fear to speak truth.

I also want to praise others more, and I am perpetually perplexed as to why it is so challenging to make compliments, because it never takes away from who I am and what I want.

I am trying to build the habit, strengthen such muscles, be more reflexive, more natural, and more forthcoming – with both spontaneous praise and with truth.

<u>Emily, 11 years old</u>: I need to speak up more. Sometimes I have good ideas or I see something that's not right, but I'm too scared to say anything. *

<u>Cristina</u>: Above everything else, I need to detangle what I want from what others seem to be desiring of me, and afterwards practice that detachment on a regular basis.

Beyond that, it is high time to admit my emotional fragility, and regularly practice being vulnerable and wholeheartedly open - an Everest-climbing endeavor if there ever was one.

And now's your turn: **What habits must I build?**

How can I strengthen my self-love?

<u>Tanya, 12 years old</u>: I love myself a lot, so I don't really think I need it. I love myself as myself, but not in a narcissistic way.

<u>Cristina</u>: Self-love is strengthened by prioritizing self-love. By discipline. By offering to the divine inside our hearts few small but regular gifts of love, which thus become gifts of self-love.

Above all, self-love is strengthened by constantly reminding myself that what works well in business (which is serving the needs of my clients and dissolving who I am into the space of solutions and service) is detrimental when it comes to my personal life.

In this dimension, I need to carve space for my own desires, remembering on a regular basis that, while wanting what others want makes for spectacular professional alignment and accelerated outcomes, my ultimate duty in this existence is to my soul. I don't want to arrive at the pearly gates to find out I failed my own mission while helping everyone else fulfill their own. That wouldn't be selflessness; that would be stupidity.

<u>John</u>: I don't know if I need to strengthen my self-love. I am constantly appreciative of what I am trying to do. I am kind to myself, and the way I love myself is more than adequate. I have come to love who I am, including my limitations and contributions.

I waste little time wishing I was someone else, and I think the most important dimension of self-love is acceptance. And while I am nowhere near done in evolving, I am focusing on loving others.

And now's your turn: **How can I strengthen my self-love?**

What help do I need most?

<u>Thalia, 12 years old</u>: I need help recognizing that I don't have to be perfect. This is definitely something I need to work on because I am a bit of a perfectionist, and I get upset when I don't do things how I intend to do them. Therefore, the help that I need is recognizing that sometimes things are not at their best, recognizing that sometimes I will be wrong, and that's OK.

<u>Emery, 17 years old</u>: I need help opening metaphorical doors to meet new people, and be exposed to new ideas and perspectives. How can I expand socially? I want to learn and do new things. I want to understand life more.

<u>John</u>: I need feedback from others, critiques on how I could better handle things, I need other people's viewpoints. Not fishing for compliments or praise, but honest assessments. Then I need help to listen to all of that with curiosity, receive the feedback, understand it, and digest it. This is the hardest part: to quiet the defense mechanisms and let the words do their magic.

<u>Cristina</u>: With each year, I seem to be getting both more afraid, and significantly less afraid, so I think that on occasion I could use some space to talk about it.

This might have something to do with experience, aging, having more to lose, and having more courage too. There's a sublimation: you start not caring about some things, while suddenly caring much more about other things. Talking about it with the right people could be useful, and I often feel a visceral need for a special context to do so with others who might relate.

With time and progress, I also notice some skin-shedding, as if there's an existential crack in my exoskeleton - that hardened shell made from expectations plus all the roles I've played on the TV of my life. And in the absence of that armor, and in the presence of the tender flesh beneath, who am I left to be, and what do I want? I need help answering these questions for myself.

And now's your turn: **What help do I need most?**

What is my philosophy for life?

<u>Cristina</u>:

1. Live an examined life, the Greek Way.

2. Have no fear of death. (Why would we fear the inevitable?)

3. If I am going to bother doing something, then I am going to take it as far as it can go.

4. To receive, I must first give, then ask for what I want, and then, eventually, harvest the thing I desire - because the gods are generous, but they never shove anything in my bag. I have to take it.

5. Love everything and everyone (even the absolute a-holes).

6. Love the world and hold central the knowledge that everything is, actually, a gift (even the absolute a-holes).

7. Make everything beautiful.

8. Leave everything better.

9. Build "it" ten times bolder than necessary; and then make "it" ten times bolder again. Whatever "it" is.

10. Plan for tomorrow but live today.

11. Do not consume myself with things I cannot control, influence, or change.

12. Take responsibility for everything.

Emery, 17 years old: I hold two concepts, like two halves in opposition to one another. One is the idea that I will spend my life doing what is right for the world, to benefit humanity for the longest time possible, in the most positive way, no matter what that costs me, and no matter what that takes. That's the goal. The other is the philosophy of contentment. I should spend the time that I have in my life doing things that I enjoy. I am trying to balance the two.

John: I believe that we're all seeking a philosophy of life, not the traditional schools such as Stoicism or the Epicureans, but a philosophy to help us understand the meaning of life.

For me writing is illuminating. Here's my personal credo: *Be myself, not what others expect. Give first without an expectation. Be present and find the positive. Seek to understand what I don't know. Pursue unconditional love. Ask for help for self and others. Listen more. Read more. Write more. Love myself but be selfless. Open my mind and heart to things that offend me. Try to have as much compassion for the perpetrators as the victims. Comfort the afflicted and afflict the comfortable. Become the best I can be, and success will follow. Be grateful for the sacrifices that have gifted me this moment. Smile and help others smile.*

Zachary, 16 years old: Go with the flow. The ability to adapt is one of the most important ways to be.

And now's your turn: **What is my philosophy of life?**

What role should my significant other play in my life?

<u>Cristina</u>: One singular role: equal and equitable partner. A companion in all things, including those empty spaces that are needed in a relationship so one could breathe, reflect, and adjust everything, from identity to goals.

I don't know if I am evolved enough to feel unconditional love, but what I do know is that I will support my partner unconditionally in whatever he needs and in whatever he is doing at any given time. While I might grumble, I will walk on glass for the things that are important to him.

When I was a kid, someone explained utopian socialism as a place where *"to each is given based on their needs, and from each is required based on their abilities"*. While we all know how the socialist experiments fared in the grander scheme of things, this formula might actually yield the secret to a fantastic relationship. I won't ask for what is not there, but I will give all that is needed, and demand to full potential. And then measure myself with the same (rather exigent, yes) yardstick.

It works splendidly.

<u>John</u>: It is youthful and idealistic to even consider the ways one's significant other is supposed to support one's life. It is proof of the fact that the central ego, of *"I"*, *"me"*, and *"mine"*, puts everybody else in the supporting cast. When I am the protagonist, my significant other's role is to support what I do and, preferably, not get in my way.

Over time, I have been trying to look at this from a different perspective, and understand how our lives are intertwined in ways that can't be separated.

I'm trying to figure out what role I, myself, play in my significant other's life. I'm not saying that's how I focus and how I live. I wish I could say that. Honestly, I think I'm still tilted toward what I want and what I hope my life partner will do for me. But it has become a more porous thought, allowing perforations in my self-absorption, and through these holes enters the light and the love that connects us.

And now's your turn: **What role should my significant other play in my life?**

What does having kids/not having kids mean to me?

<u>Tanya, 12 years old</u>: I don't know, I am little. When I am older, yes, because having kids is having tiny people around, and who doesn't want tiny people in their lives?

<u>John</u>: I've had impassioned debates with people about *"what might be the meaning of life if you're not going to have children?"* I remember having a dogmatic point of view: that procreation is part of our responsibility. That everyone must seriously consider having children.

Today, I believe this has to be in one's life the most sober, focused, and intentional decision possible. For it is a responsibility that cannot be undone. As with all forks in the road, we must decide, and find a partner who subscribes to the same vision - a house cannot be divided on this issue.

<u>Zachary, 16 years old</u>: Money versus no money.

<u>Cristina</u>: I support your reproductive autonomy. Whatever is right for you, is right for you, and you shouldn't have to justify it to anyone.

Skip the family Thanksgiving dinners if they prove uncomfortable! Do you have five kids and people say *"sheesh, have you ever heard of birth control?"* Fuck these people. Do you have no kids and people say *"have you thought about kids?"* Fuck these people too.

I long for a society with a bit more tact. Especially because many can't do what they want when it comes to children: some want them, and can't have them, some don't want them and can't prevent having them, plus everything in between. Let's have more tact, please.

Ever since I was a teenager, I knew I didn't want children. I didn't like children. I didn't have patience for children. I considered that I have already paid my child-rearing dues to society by raising my 6 younger siblings. And I deeply believed that this planet doesn't need yet one more human to support (which I still feel).

Around the age of 33 or so, I changed my mind, and that's perfectly acceptable; a person has the right to change their mind on this topic.

Today, I love being a mother, and I am glad I gave myself the experience of childbirth, while knowing full well that I would have also been perfectly happy either way.

Also, I wanted to use my reproductive choice to make a small statement: have just one child. I know, not a new idea, but an idea which, at scale, could give our global society more than 50% reduction in population in one generation. While intensely personal, this might solve the grand challenges faced by our world today!

Was it a sacrifice to have just one child? Yes. But my choice is an example that we can make decisions which could result in goodness for the planet through peaceful and selfless means.

Bottom line: depending on what stage of my life I would have had to answer it, I would have given radically different answers to this question.

You do you, my friend.

And now's your turn: **What does having kids/not having kids mean to me?**

How long should my accomplishments last?

Thalia, 12 years old: It depends on the accomplishment, as long as that's not what I am going to be always talking about. It is important to celebrate yourself: *"hey, I did that!"* It really depends on how much it means to me, rather than how much it means to my family, or my friends. It is kinda different for everyone.

John: They should last as long as they are useful. Hard stop.

What I do is ephemeral, fleeting, and evaporating, propelling other things forward. While I know that my "accomplishments" ideally change things around me, I can never fully appreciate how it all weaves with the flow of time, nature, and the universal stream of molecules.

Everything is simply part of the great currents that have preceded me and will follow me. I have no interest in people remembering my name after I die. I have tried to generate good energy through my presence and deeds, and that adds anonymously to the endless river of life.

Cristina: In an uncharacteristic streak of humbleness, I don't imagine anything I accomplish to be significant, simply because most things are not. I am a pragmatist. Once I am dead, it won't matter to me anyway.

On a daily basis, I aim to be kind and gentle with my kid, to tread lightly into the world, to love as much as possible, and create as much as possible. To lovingly fold laundry. None of that lasts, but maybe it does in the hearts of those I love.

And now's your turn: **How long should my accomplishments last?**

When should I change?

<u>Luca, 15 years old</u>: The moment you say it! If you say *"I want to change"* then you also say, even if just subtext, *"I want to start now"*. These two things are connected. And if you don't start now, there is a high chance that you'll never start. Therefore, the answer is: now.

<u>John</u>: The right time to change is like fishing, watching for a shooting star, or meeting your true love: it would be great if we could schedule it! Sadly, it's not how it works.

Either we change or we don't, we just continue to age, the seasons keep unfolding, so does the calendar, and the orbits of Earth around the Sun. Every moment of each such cycle is different: the flow of the air, the water, the temperature, the inhabitants, everything is different and transforming the trillions of cells in the body. Every month we have new skin, and new pathways in the brain, morphed by our learning and experiences.

Our very existence reminds me of the *Ship of Theseus* thought experiment, about whether an object, after having had all of its original components replaced, remains the same object. A question was raised by ancient philosophers: after several hundreds of years of maintenance, if each individual part of the *Ship of Theseus* was replaced, one at a time, was it still the same ship?

So, if all our cells are new, are we the same ship? We are constantly changing physically, spiritually, and emotionally. Either we accept it, or not. And yet, as we gain insights, we realize there's something very solid and stable within us, even when everything else is changing around us.

<u>Cristina:</u> When who we are is no longer fitting our goals, no longer fitting our identity, no longer fitting our pants, then it is time to change. Admit the need for change, make a plan, then work the plan.

And when we derail from it (which we will, unless we are not human), let's go back to the plan, adjust, adapt, and squish the doubt that creeps its ugly, disruptive head. Then, we keep walking. Keep doing. Keep changing because we will anyway, so might as well change in a way that will make us love ourselves more.

And now's your turn: **When should I change?**

For what will I risk a broken heart?

<u>Luca, 15 years old</u>: To go that far, it would have to be important.

<u>Cristina</u>: My heart is worth risking my heart. Sophism? Perhaps. But let's be real: the thing most worth breaking the heart is the heart itself. I would do anything for love, and probably so would you.

I would risk it for dreams worth dreaming, even if I will never achieve them. For the future which we cannot see, but would love to co-create. For the magnificent privilege of feeling alive.

<u>John</u>: None of us wants a broken heart and would do much to avoid such a feeling, while knowing full well that our hearts will be broken over and over again. Avoidance of such an experience is rejection of real life. A broken heart is evidence that we can aim for a magnificent future in which to invest ourselves fully.

Some may say it's naïve and irrational to risk that kind of emotional consequence. I've come to believe in the desirability of a broken heart. If I am passionate about it, my heart will be both broken and broken open. Then healed by time, perspective, and the satisfaction that I went for it!

Hearts are meant to be broken so they can become bigger and stronger, so they could love more, and appreciate the opportunity. The people we love will die. And the causes we care about will not be solved. We will have unreasonable expectations. And our own deepest disappointments will also, of course, break our hearts. But a broken heart is, by definition, an open heart. That is worth the risk.

And now's your turn: **For what will I risk a broken heart?**

Fall

What is Fall?

Reflection. Change. Harvest.

Seeing the fruits of our labor.

How do I know what's true?

<u>Lily, 15 years old</u>: My red could be blue for you. But we both just call it red because that's what we've been trained to say. Truth is rarely just straight truth because everyone has different perceptions. It's really hard to just make something true or false because there are layers to it. And you can't just label something 'good' or 'bad'. Because often there's layers to that as well. Until today, I have not realized how truth is not actually real.

<u>John</u>: In our mind, in our heart, we know when something is true. Something that feels authentic, real, and important is self-evident. There are so many facades, a labyrinth of lies, a maze of misrepresentation, and the truth can be hiding in plain sight. In absence of any absolute tools for assessment, like in most everything, what's true starts within us.

<u>Tanya, 12 years old</u>: I don't know what is true, but I trust what I trust, and if it's wrong, well, then I will learn a lesson, and in learning, now I know what's true. Simple!

<u>Cristina</u>: Instinct is always a good barometer, especially when combined with research, education, and perpetual hunger for facts. Atop that, grafting a commitment for self-reflection seems to help, as well as having a practice of inquiry instead of pontification, and an open mind that operates with a vigilant eye towards truth decay.

Ultimately, once we pass some frontiers of knowing, we have to purely accept that we don't know what's true. How could a subject trapped in a photograph know what is outside the frame? If we go even further, to spiritual realms or quantum dimensions, the answers become even less clear, and yet, every day we need to get out of bed and move on.

Beyond this psychological and philosophical level, what is true
is that media is foremost entertainment (not knowledge),
politics is foremost a scoreboard (not administration), money is
foremost a collective agreement (not value), and every moment
of my life I have choices to govern or be governed. What is true
is that freedom is terrifying and yet, so glorious. So much of
truth is personal truth.

And now's your turn: **How do I know what's true?**

Where in my life do I have complete faith?

<u>Lily, 15 years old:</u> My family loves me. Evolution is real. Gravity is real. I feel like faith is different from truth. Faith is what you believe, not what you think.

<u>Cristina</u>: Having complete faith in the goodness and heuristics of existence is key. I trust the laws of evolutionary biology that got me here, the laws that push me to advance and preserve my own life and that of my offspring. The rules that are nudging from the inside, incentivizing us to play ball with fellow humans because we need each other.

I have complete faith in what I have chiseled myself into being, in the habits I have built, and the discipline instilled inside. More importantly, I have complete faith that others, just like me, are trained by what Mother Nature tells us to do with subtle but inexorable hints.

<u>John</u>: Many of our sacred cows have been drawn and quartered. We are regularly subjected to *"avalanches from the top of Mount Grace"* and I'm not sure who said it, but it's hard to be cynical enough.

The bonfire of our skepticism burns with the many logs of our loyalty, plus the fuel of former facts. Complete faith has been going up in smoke, and maybe that's good. Perhaps it's not important to have complete faith in anything. Complete faith is dangerous, and our skepticism, inquiries, and sobriety can serve us well. A bit of discomfort will keep us all honest, questioning the simple story we apply to an unknowable world. Let's appreciate how absurd complete faith can be when ambiguity is in far greater supply.

And now's your turn: **Where in my life do I have complete faith?**

In which ways is my life out of balance?

<u>Maria, 15 years old</u>: I feel like the amount of time I'm spending thinking about myself versus thinking about other people is really out of whack. I spend a lot of time thinking about what other people are doing, what other people look like, what other people said. I tend to hyper-focus on people that have things that I want. I really don't think about myself, what I have, and what qualities I like about myself. I think that balance is really off.

<u>John</u>: A good life is beautifully well-lopsided. Work needs you, you gotta work. Family needs you. You go to your family. Yep, there are times when both need you, and life is super-lopsided. But you gotta make choices: what kind of work, and what kind of family, and how do you do that? It's not a balancing act, per se. It's adapting. It is about making adjustments, which, by the way, may mean a different career, a different city, a different school district, a different environment.

Yeah, life is probably out of balance because it's too balanced.

<u>Andrea, 16 years old</u>: My personal life and my social life are out of balance. An imbalance between the relationships I hold in each. My personal life is so heavy while my social life is very light.

<u>Cristina</u>: A decade ago, John asked me this question and opened my eyes to the idea that, perhaps, being out of balance is a natural state. Once we look at it that way, we stop wasting energy to correct the imbalance, redirecting time and effort towards understanding.

Ever since I gave up on the idea of balance, I actually feel better, and I squeeze so much more out of my years.

Forget balance! Let's be who we are, unapologetically. Gloriously askew. Uniquely ourselves, ferociously bright, unrelentingly happy, and mesmerizing to watch.

And now's your turn: **In which ways is my life out of balance?**

When am I stuck?

<u>Lily, 15 years old</u>: I feel stuck relative to the state of the world. And I feel very small because I know things are happening and I can't stop them. I'm trying, but I know that my trying is not going to fix the big problems of the planet.

<u>John</u>: Being stuck is really just a state of mind. We think we have plenty of time so we wait, which can get us stuck.

While taking every ride in the amusement park can provide revelatory information, it can also be a delaying tactic fueled by the illusion that something better might show up. Stuck-ness is procrastination. It is inaction. We have to trust our curiosity and instincts. But let's always pick a date to move, to experiment, to decide. Take micro-steps, little acts, to start the flywheel of change. A deadline and some motion will liberate us.

<u>Cristina</u>: I am stuck when I am narrow-minded and stubborn, which must be, hands down, the least attractive human trait in existence. And when I am stuck, there are two medicines I can take: commitment and rest.

Feeling stuck signals that I need to put more energy into it. When I feel like stepping out, it is actually a moment to step in. Counterintuitive, but that commitment always gets me unstuck

And then I rest, because when the weary soul, the weary mind, and the weary body get some rest, the stuck-ness often goes away. Resting provides the blank page for new ideas to come. And when new ideas flow, the way out appears.

And now's your turn: **When am I stuck?**

Have I paid my dues?

<u>Tanya, 12 years old</u>: For what I have, I think so, maybe? But I still have to work at it because I am only a child so I owe so much to my family. As a momentary state of affairs, let's go with "yes" because I try to really enjoy being a kid.

<u>Cristina</u>: You pay to play, my friend, over and over, and better pay it swiftly, because not paying is not playing, and that's worse. Paying dues is the immutable human condition.

There's a tax levied on our mortality by having started in the mailroom, by grieving at a funeral stone, by looking at the white hair multiplying.

As a woman, there is also a tax paid as I carve yet another notch on the prison wall of patriarchy while I keep my mouth shut and my blood is demanding air time. Among other things.

When young, the fee is often small; when old, fates hike the price. We hurt because we love, because we dream, because we are creators. The dues we pay are quantum energy exchanged for the privilege to build.

I am gladly paying it, and I do it daily.

<u>John</u>: There is an archaic concept that once one finishes their apprenticeship, after hard work and the investment of an appropriate amount of time, they should be granted tenure because they "paid their dues". That antiquated expectation aside, I believe that our dues will never be paid up! The world is changing so fast that few can rely on the education, competences, and achievements of the past to lead them into the future. No one can afford nowadays to pay their dues and be done.

In 1632, Robert Burton said: *"Give cheerfully. Pay thy dues willingly. Be not a slave to thy mony."* He was advancing the concept of never-ending dues paying, and highlighting our moral obligation to support and finance the common good, as compassionate card-carrying members of the human race.

Once we expand our thinking, dues paying becomes a mindset of gratitude, towards all the sacrifices other people made so we could be here. Our ancestors, and also complete strangers, paid their dues so we could benefit. They made investments in things we take for granted - from voting rights to education, medicine, and much more.

For all the opportunities we want the next generations to enjoy tomorrow, we must cheerfully pony up our dues today.

And now's your turn: **Have I paid my dues?**

What is my strongest prejudice?

<u>Andrea, 16 years old:</u> I am very judgy. Freshmen. When I see them. They haven't done anything to me, but I don't like them. I have nothing against them. But they are clueless. They don't know how anything works. For some reason, I don't like them.

<u>Cristina</u>: *"If I can do it, everyone can. And probably everyone should".* That's my deepest prejudice towards others.

A lifetime ago, one of my mentors drilled into my consciousness that the most heinous modern crime is to blame the poor for being poor. I sometimes did that, yes, and it transformed me to see the wrongness of it.

Two weeks ago, I found myself unexpectedly separated from my sunglasses, which is difficult because sensitivity to light is a perpetually painful affair. Pressed by necessity, I stepped into a local thrift store and bought myself a pair.

Fast forward another week, I met with a friend whose economics have always been bootstrapped. Incidentally, this friend was in dire need of sunglasses. *"Here, you can have mine!"* I offered the new pair, by then having been reunited with the original glasses. *"No thanks, they are ugly!"* the friend said vehemently. It shook me.

I asked *"Are you sure you don't want the sunglasses?"* *"Nope! They are too ugly and I would rather squint than wear them."*

I am still chewing on this exchange.

Ugly glasses? Bring them on! I accept them with grace because I would rather look ugly than suffer. Difficult problems? I approach them with grace because I know I can bend my ego, growing and learning in the process. My strongest prejudice is that mutual grace can solve it all, that it can be done because I obviously do it all that time, that everything would be possible if only people would choose to stretch, accept the context, shape solutions, and push through the murkiness of who they are towards who they could become. Doing this, we could solve, at scale, poverty and so many other things. As I said, it's a strong prejudice.

<u>John</u>: *"I am different and so special, so exceptional and so much more deserving than other people!"* I believe this to be the basis, the foundation, the root, of all our prejudices.

We are raised with the notion that our family, our tribe, our team, our country are better. Not just marginally better, but morally better. And this mindset and perspective gets deeply ingrained. My choices, my affiliations, my path is then inherently superior because I am me.

Our egos manipulate our minds and action, blocking learning, curiosity, and mutual understanding. In its wrongness, ego reduces the world to a one dimensional, nearly comical world, of *"us"* and *"them"*. *"Good guys"* and *"bad guys"*.

I have to fight this. I have to fight the intellectually dishonest inclination to instantly label others with brutal prejudice only so I could elevate my standing. When I manage to see beyond my supersonic judgmentalism, I see a different world. A world that breaks open the simpleton narratives I have nurtured into stories. A world where my little ego dissolves into the connection I share with people and places I have compartmentalized - enjoying, and enhancing the remarkable diversity that endows nature and the human world around me.

And now's your turn: **What is my strongest prejudice?**

Where am I going?

<u>Tanya, 12 years old</u>: Somewhere. Definitely somewhere. Could go really in many directions. But definitely somewhere, towards the future.

<u>John</u>: I'm reminded of a dance I had with my young cousin Marna. At her wedding, she asked Uncle John, as she calls me, to join her on the dance floor. As we were dancing, beaming with beauty, she said: *"Uncle John, I'm so happy. My life is going exactly as I planned it"*. I tried to listen: *"What is your plan?"*. She says: *"Married by 25. Check. We'll have our first baby at 27, second baby at 29."* And she carried on to her retirement date at age 65, including where she was going to be traveling afterwards!

My mind was whirling and my hair was standing up at the back of my neck. I stopped dancing: *"Marna, I love you and I'm so happy for you. Let's enjoy today. The plan should be to enjoy this moment, right now."* And she said, *"You don't like my plan?"* I said, *"It's not that I don't like your plan. I just don't think you should be planning right now."* Marna became upset, wishing I would just accept her plan, and my wife had to separate us.

Eighteen months after our conversation, my cousin went through a very difficult divorce. Four years later, I was invited back to a second wedding, and Marna asked me to dance again.

I went up there with my lips sealed. She grabbed my face and said: *"No day goes by that I don't think about the dance we had and I'm very happy, enjoying this moment. I appreciate not having a plan. I don't care where life takes me from this point forward. I just want to enjoy every minute of it."* The good thing is, Marna still dances with me.

<u>Cristina:</u> I am getting redundant perhaps, but here you have it: where am I going? Always too far.

If most of the time I am NOT wondering if I am going too far, then I must be playing it safe, scared, and below my potential.

Action, vision, emotion, are seldom about range, and often about scale. Humans are not particularly good at adjusting action to the scale that most outcomes require, so I am interested in all peaks that can be climbed, in the edges and trenches and canyons of existence, be them inner or outer, not because medals await at the top, but because the canyons exist, and thus, so do I.

The edge validates the journey.

And now's your turn: **Where am I going?**

What difference will I make?

<u>John</u>: The difference we might make is unspoken, deeply submerged under our self-importance.

Steve Jobs said *"We're here to put a dent in the universe. Otherwise, why else even be here?"*

The difference I can make is in every moment. It is not connected to fame, with my name on a building, or personal wealth. What we do and how we live changes lives. Making a difference is a decision to do good things when no one is looking; to live fully aligned with our superpowers, because it's what we can do.

It is the energy of our goodwill. It is the way I love and help others learn to love. Making a difference is leading a life that focuses on that living and on that loving.

That's a dent that will be felt and carried on.

<u>Cruz, 9 years old</u>: I hope to one day invent a machine that can turn broccoli into chocolate. That would make a HUGE difference in the world, right? *

<u>Emily, 11 years old:</u> I hope I can protect the environment. Maybe I'll become a scientist when I grow up, and find ways to save the planet from climate change. *

<u>Cristina</u>: We make the biggest difference when we subject ourselves to the push of the world - what it needs from us, the corners it crams us in, the things we do kicking and screaming only to realize, later on, that it was the best thing that could have happened.

Some of the difference we make is nestled in the pull of the heart; in the voices we hear in our souls when the room is quiet. In the opportunities that surface when we least expect, the jobs we get recruited for, and the jobs we fail to get. The friend that asks for help in the middle of the night, the stranger we see confused on the sidewalk, and the pets we rescue. The books we read and the books we don't read. The paths we take and the doors we don't open.

Everything makes a difference to something. Every day. Every hour.

We have to actively head towards the future, while simultaneously building our own roads necessary for advancement. It's slow going, but what else is there?

On my deathbed as I look back, I want to see that I did all I could, and for that journey, intention matters perhaps more than results. We could tirelessly work on water scarcity, cybersecurity, democracy, gender, or governance. Whatever. With time, the topics change, but the intentions remain. What difference will I make? All I can, and as much as I can. Every day.

And now's your turn: **What difference will I make?**

Do I really want less change?

<u>Evelyn, 16 years old</u>: Change means something unexpected, something good or bad. Change makes life fun. If my life was a straight line I would not learn how to adapt. I would be really bored.

<u>John</u>: Of course not. The more we accept change and help it along, the more satisfaction we experience.

When we think about it, the truth is that we really want everything to change. Everything. Our standards of living, the state of the world, the happiness index of our children, our communities and our relationships.

We all experience constant, internal resistance to change, to learning a new software, acclimating to a new boss, or switching dental plans. These are inconvenient. But the more we cling, the more we feel the friction and life chafes against our domesticity.

Outside of our little comfort zones, join me and come sing together the chorus of life: *"We need change! We love change!"*

Oh, that sounds amazing!

<u>Cristina:</u> You won't hear me bitch about this because I do love change.

For lack of a Pygmalion to shape me, I have to self-serve that chisel to carve my flaws out, or shape them into assets. Beyond that, to fight change is folly. I'm too much of an Alpha to go to battle within wars with no chance of victory. And nobody wins the battle with perpetual change.

And now's your turn: **Do I really want less change?**

When is the right time?

<u>Tanya, 12 years old</u>: If it's something I want to do, the right time is exactly when I feel like it. If it's something I have to do, like chores, then, the right time to do it is ten minutes later.

<u>John</u>: I've always been struck by this quote from James Baldwin: *"the challenge is in every moment, and the time is always now."*

When we are present and not held back by what has happened or what could happen, we see what needs to be done, and yes, the right time for anything is, indeed, now. I don't mean that we should be pulling the levers of decisions in this exact microscopic moment, but we should always be moving ourselves forward, and not wallowing in analysis or overthinking our actions.

There is no other time. Where we are is the only time we can count on. Now is the moment to take the next step toward what we want, and if we tiptoe or take big flying leaps is less important than actually doing it now.

<u>Cristina</u>: Now. The right time is now.

Now, now, now, now, now. Probably now. Most likely now. And if not "now" don't blink, because it's coming.

Seriously speaking, most of our lives we are either "too young" for something or "too old" for something. If neither of these things are true, then most likely, we are "not ready" for that something.

I used to joke that in a woman's life there must be a single, mythical day when she's neither too young nor too old. A DAY. Not a year, not a decade; no. One day.

And before that day comes, everyone will tell you that you are too young. Then the day arrives, and you, of course, don't recognize it as such, so it passes unheralded, and un-actioned-upon, therefore pushing you unceremoniously into the "holy-buckets-I-better-hurry" category because, suddenly, it's getting clear that you are swiftly becoming too old for that thing for which two days prior, you were too young.

I wish I was joking.

And now's your turn: **When is the right time?**

Am I on the right path?

<u>Luca, 15 years old</u>: Yes, I think I am on the right path, mixing the stuff that I need to do with the stuff that I like to do. I believe this balance is a good way to approach the right path in life.

<u>John</u>: Yes.

There is no other path. We are at this place and this moment. This is where we are meant to be. No regret, no "what if" or "what should have been" will make a difference. That rumination will only steal time and energy from the present.

Joseph Campbell said: *If you see your path laid out in front of you step by step, you know it's not your path. Your own path you make with every step you take. That's why it's your path.*

This path, no matter how ugly or beautiful, is the only possible path from now to the next thing.

<u>Cristina:</u> I am inclined to think that the environment will let me know: if what I am doing is working, if I see acceleration in the direction I am pursuing, then I take it to mean that yes, I must be on the right path.

If I get pushed inside dark alleys and constantly smash my head on the upper threshold, if countless doors close in my face, that's feedback from the Universe asking me to reconsider my journey.

It's tricky though, I will admit, because sometimes the path simply needs more persistence, longer timeframes, some trials and tribulations as proof of serious intent. We periodically underestimate the shortness of our existence.

I work with people who have dedicated their personal and professional lives to much needed crusades. Such people, while patron saints in their fields, are facing their 70's and 80's with bitterness and doubt: *"am I on the right path?"*

Of course they are! Undoubtedly so.

But the work often goes beyond one's lifespan, and it's disheartening indeed. How might we make peace with the gods when the path, while obviously right, proves nevertheless to be longer than our finite, human life?

It's a difficult conundrum of purpose.

Whatever it is for you though, don't think too much about it. You'll bruise your knees, and when the time comes you might be stopped in your tracks, or you'll be dead. One of the two. And until one of these things happens, assume you are indeed, on the right path.

Just go!

And now's your turn: **Am I on the right path?**

What would my childhood self say about me today?

<u>Tanya, 12 years old</u>: My younger self would look at my art, and yell "how the heck did you achieve that?' Something along these lines. I have been sculpting since I was little, but I didn't think I would get into sculpting the way I am into it right now. And today I am becoming really good at it, which would be surprising for that younger version of myself.

<u>Cristina</u>: It's simple. That kid would say: *"how marvelous to have these foods to eat, then be all you can be in sweet America!"*

Her eyes would sparkle. Hands would swish over the clothes I wear on my now-body, and rejoice. Would think me fat, dance amidst books, then pat my back for explorations, homes and Jedi powers, friends, money, scale of thought, and beautiful adventures.

She would be proud of many things, annoyed at few, would miss our dad as I do too, and arch a brow on why nobody told her all she should have known so long ago. Would love my daughter and the dog, be shy around my husband, breathe in the greed for life, for world, for art, for giving, aim for the asteroids-of-possible, and ask me earnestly: *"What else is there? I like you. Now, let's go!"*

<u>John</u>: The introvert John that I was in 4th grade was really struggling with his identity, wanting to belong and be accepted while yearning to immerse himself in the social world.

That little boy would be pretty pleased with how I engage with the community and how I express myself today as a recovering introvert. He would have hoped I was famous by now, so perhaps that aspect might be a tad disappointing.

I learned how to be a son then, but I did not think much about being a dad. My father would shake hands with me when saying "good night!" We had a good connection, but a literal, "arm's length" relationship. Today my childhood self would see me in my capacity as a dad, he might notice my comfort with intimacy and expressing love openly. I think he would like that.

I have a quote on my wall that I wrote when I was 9: *"A good leader is willing to follow rules and suggest rules."* It is funny when I read it, because it is incredibly mature, and also fully idealistic. We have to give due credit to the kids we were, and today isn't just the young-me that would have things to say to the now-me, but the other way around too. I would take a moment to tell John how the seeds of the future were there before drawing breath, revealed over and over during our life.

And now's your turn: **What would my childhood self say about me today?**

What is the most frequent argument my mind and my heart have with each other?

<u>Luca, 15 years old</u>: *"Is this the right thing to do, or should I do something else?"*

<u>John</u>: If we are lucky the heart and the mind have a healthy relationship, soothing and provoking one another on a daily basis. It's a constant debate, and often, a wrestling match aiming to understand what's real, aligned, and true.

The messages that our mind receives from the environment perpetually muzzle, mute, and silence the heart, prioritizing survival and getting by.

To see the healthy space of existence requires not just turning off the radio of the mind, but also trying to discern the frequency of truth amidst the media pollution, and actively combat the interference of our apathetic tendencies. Otherwise, we'll end up muddling through. Settling. Compromising. Most significantly, we end up unfulfilled. And when that happens, the trenches between the heart and the mind are where I need to be, allowing the friction to awaken me to who and what I am.

<u>Cristina</u>: My mind and my heart fight about one thing and one thing only: identity.

For example, I know this is completely ridiculous, idiotic, and not particularly practical, but my heart wants me to buy a home in the country of my birth. While it will grow in value long-term, the truth is that it is a stupid yearning.

Yet, here it is, the heart screaming from the top of its nonexistent lungs, and quite explicitly throwing at my mind, like lumps of clay, chunks of ancestry, bits of culture, tangible Romanian art, intangible traditions, plus the symbolic act of ownership towards the land where predecessors have left their bones.

In good old American fashion, whatever history I don't have, I can buy, right? In the meantime, my mind is yelling from the rafters as to how dumb and utterly cliche this is, judging this desire of the heart to be akin to the instincts of a salmon being driven up river kicking and screaming the whole way.

Guess who is winning?

And now's your turn: **What is the most frequent argument
my mind and my heart have with each other?**

If I know I could do it, why am I scared of doing it?

<u>Evelyn, 13 years old:</u> I would be less afraid. Afraid of being me.

<u>John</u>: We live in a world that gives us few opportunities to experience real fears. We have an overabundance of choices and infinite options. We cloistered in comfort. We can skirt angst by avoiding all challenges altogether. At the other end of the spectrum, we also have few cliffs from which we need to leap. Given this, my greatest fear is living in a world of self-deception rife with paths of least resistance, forgetting who we truly are and who we can be.

I want to face adventure and the exhilaration of the unknown. I have to quiet the bullies of doubt. I have to jump into the moment, and allow my potential to be freed from intellectual brake pads. There is no time to waiver. To face whatever fear I have left, I need to test the possibilities of truth.

<u>Cristina</u>: I am pretty sure that when we are scared of doing things, that's just trauma talking in our heads, objecting to the possibility of success.

When that "scared" feeling comes, it is just a manifestation of the ingrained belief that everything should come only from hard work. Maybe my immigrant self still believes immigrants could only go so far. Or maybe I am still hearing the voices of the dictators that ruled the land of my birth and told me, and all those alive then, that we were "worthless worms". I didn't think they were right, but one cannot unhear it.

Maybe the system itself brainwashes and persuades. Maybe I don't want "it" hard enough. Maybe every time I do one of those "next level" things, the person I was before doing them dies, and I am scared of that little death. But I do it anyway.

And now's your turn: **If I know I could do it, why am I scared of doing it?**

Why am I bored?

<u>Camille, 12 years old</u>: I think boredom is just my brain's way of saying 'slow down!' *

<u>John</u>: Boredom stalks us like a prey animal, feeding on superficiality over depth.

It is so hard to go deep into anything anymore. Like an aspiring college student, I am inclined to audit life instead of taking it for full credit. I get numb. My attention is overloaded. I literally get turned off to what's going on in the world, suffering from an ongoing and massive human hangover, nauseous and undernourished on the empty calories of a brutal and vicious cycle that feeds on itself.

I love this Buddhist insight: *"If you are bored of something, you have not done it long enough."* and I think we should try to remember its truth, persisting just a little bit more when bored. It is important to lose ourselves inside the boredom, so we can find ourselves, our flow, and the sense of wonder and enjoyment that's always inside our chest cavity. If nothing else, because being bored too easily makes us boring people.

<u>Cristina</u>: "Bored" is a dirty, entitled, and very lazy word. I consider boredom somewhere between murder and incest on the list of sins. How could anyone be bored when the world is so nuanced, generous, rife with problems to solve and messes to clean up, abundant with entertainment, and always thought-provoking?

Most relevant to this boredom question, I like the "me" on the inside of me. When I am just with "me", I am with my best friend - we might argue, we might not see eye to eye, but we are always good company. Me being with me in solitude and without outside stimuli is not torture to be transcended, but a gift. I am never bored.

And now's your turn: **Why am I bored?**

What is my blindspot?

<u>Cristina</u>: I don't know.

I constantly ask for feedback, and perpetually eavesdrop on my husband's conversation with his family and friends, trying to glimpse those pesky blindspots.

I know I don't know. I know I don't even know myself fully. How is one supposed to know something we cannot even physically see without mirrors and other objects which we needed to create? It's tricky.

But it is - perhaps - the knowing that those blindspots exist, and the trying to see them, that counts.

<u>Evelyn, 16 years old</u>: I am very easily fooled by people. Whether it's a simple joke or lies. I want to believe in the goodness of people, to be more aware. But it is a struggle.

<u>John</u>: We constantly live in the dangerous zone between confidence and overconfidence, subjective and often wrong about what we see and don't see, or how we interpret things in the blink of an eye. It's arrogant. This zone is where stereotypes live and prosper, where rush to judgments and superficial information dominate the mind, efficient but inaccurate.

I think my biggest blind spot is thinking I don't have blind spots. Believing that I am very perceptive, and deluding myself that I am careful in how I interpret what's around me. That is the height of myopia: believing that we "get it", that we see it all, when in fact, we never do.

And now's your turn: **What is my blindspot?**

Can I love unconditionally?

<u>Luca, 15 years old:</u> No, I don't think I can love without asking anything in return. I wish I could; I am being honest.

<u>Tanya, 12 years old</u>: Yes. I have a dog! We love each other unconditionally.

<u>John:</u> "Unconditionally" is a high bar - no conditions, no reservation, no expectations.

I, myself, made vows of unconditional love when I married my soulmate. But if I believe that I am loving unconditionally, I am completely deceiving myself, because regardless of what I consciously believe, I do seem to accumulate micro-conditions, wishing on regular basis that our relationship was different, that my wife was a bit different, and overall, that I could reshape events and another human into something different and more to my liking.

The truth is, that the more we experience life as a parent, as a partner, as a friend, the more we have to abandon the desire for the Svengali/Pygmalion magical powers to chisel others into the image we have in our heads, giving up the craving to make them into what they are not.

We can love unconditionally if we are willing to surrender the ego, to see the other until there is no "other." This is a difficult task, and a constant battle to love what and who exists.

<u>Cristina</u>: Technically, yes, it is possible, because I have a dog, and he seems to elicit a hefty measure of unconditional love on my part. Everything and everyone else? Hard to say.

I do not feel that I have a criterion for "unconditional love" and this prevents me from accurately measuring it. I know that I am taking pleasure and beauty out of being in the glorious gardens of England at high summer, but I do not know if that is a form of conditional, or unconditional love. Maybe loving the garden is a transactional affair of the heart, because the garden is giving me beauty and lushness. Maybe it is unconditional, because I love the garden in any season… I don't know.

When it comes to humans, I am not going to even touch this garden analogy, because I think that in matters of the heart, we are concomitantly transactional and non-transactional, conditional and unconditional.

Thank goodness for the dog!

And now's your turn: **Can I love unconditionally?**

What have I learned from my biggest mistake?

<u>Cristina</u>: That wrong is wrong, even if you don't get caught!

When I was a kid, I stole my grandmother's pension. I only wanted a tiny bit of money for some childhood desire I don't even recall, and certainly I didn't need to steal the whole thing, but I figured that it would increase the chances of being found if I stole just a little bit. Grandma would certainly know that there was less in the small cardboard box she was hiding behind the heater. Thus, I stole the entire box, presumably to incite doubt: was it, indeed, stolen? Or was it misplaced?

I burned the box in the furnace and blended the cash with whatever cash I had to destroy the evidence. I am pretty sure I didn't even buy the toy in the end for fear of being caught, so technically it was all absolutely for nothing.

I still have nightmares about depriving an old widow of her income for a whole month because of an irrelevant desire, and I have never forgiven myself. I can only continuously atone. Sorry Grand Mama!

<u>Joshua, 13 years old</u>: Trying to eat an entire jar of pickles in one sitting is a big mistake. Sometimes, even if something tastes good, too much of a good thing can make you really sick. *

<u>John</u>: I once heard a prominent political figure state *"I think my biggest mistake is still ahead of me."* And while that's a cute answer to entertain the constituency, I am riveted by the idea of making bigger and bigger mistakes.

I am very attracted to the idea of growing our inner capacity to take risks, and strengthening our practice of increasingly doing so over time.

Even if we have a lot more to lose as time goes on, we also have a lot more to gain, and in taking bigger risks and making bigger

mistakes, if we learn anything, if we grow, if we accumulate
wisdom or knowledge along the way, then it is essential to make
bigger and bigger mistakes.

And now's your turn: **What have I learned from my biggest mistake?**

How do I want to be loved?

<u>Emery, 17 years old</u>: Love is beyond romance. Love is a binding force that defines my sense of community, a binding force between humans. Love defines things: *"this is a family". "This is a neighborhood". "This is a city". "This is a country."* What ends up being created through the alchemy of love is the thing that turns the force of one into two, into three, into however many people there are in the family, or group.

And that force of love is the foundation on which any organized action can take place that is more than an individual. I want to be truly cared for by others until I know that they pay attention to my physical and mental wellbeing. Until I know that they care about the same goals that I do. That they care about working together and what I stand for, and are willing to support me in these things.

<u>John</u>: Love means being surrounded by emotional, and spiritual support, by caretaking, and a generous non-judgmental swaddling of acceptance. I do not want to be loved for my potential. During my prolonged phase of arrogance, I did this to others, falling in love with what I thought would emerge. I learned the hard way that people don't ever really change for others. They only change for themselves. Today, I want to be loved (not needed) for who I am, not who I'm going to be, not who I should be. For who I am. I hope I love that way now.

<u>Cristina</u>: Actually, romance IS great. And I want to be loved with words. With balanced imbalance, joy, closeness, and nuance of feeling. With gratitude for who I am and what I create. With interest in what I do and why I am doing it. With affection, touch, and expressed emotions. With reciprocation.

I want to be loved in spades. Don't you?

And now's your turn: **How do I want to be loved?**

What is depleting my energy?

<u>Evelyn, 16 years old</u>: So many negative thoughts. When I am super negative, I am unmotivated to do anything. I feel stuck. I feel horrible about myself. I am trying to figure out how to avoid this feeling.

<u>John</u>: Suffering over which I have no control, despair regarding wars, poverty, malnutrition, and diseases. I try to put these in a very careful and conspicuous place on the shelves of my mind. I have to get closer to the challenge I have control over. Proximate to the reality that pushes my discomfort buttons. Energy comes from the source, so I must physically and intellectually approach the issue. I don't want to retreat into my own skull kingdom of doom and gloom, because that's the cause of much of my energy depletion.

By directly confronting these depletions and converting them from thoughts into actions, I get hope. Hope comes from the doing, from being part of the solution. This gives my heart solace and energizes me for the future.

<u>Cristina</u>: A few years ago, I took a test as part of a professional group I attend on occasion, and that test unexpectedly revealed that I possess minimal stores of physical and mental energy for tasks which I have spent my professional life honing into a pinnacle of excellence. In contrast, I can be thrown into work with complex and weird challenges no human has had to deal with before, and I get energized. Go figure!

Ergo, let's do mostly the things we were born to do. For this, *"Know Thyself"* is a must, because misalignment between myself and myself, or between myself and the context, kicks my energy shins every time.

We have to be honest: who we are, what we are meant to do, what we want to do... Everything else is carrying water uphill.

And now's your turn: **What is depleting my energy?**

What needs to stop for my life to really go?

<u>Tanya, 12 years old</u>: I am lucky. I don't see any barriers in my life at the moment.

<u>Cristina</u>: When I work, I believe in everything that I deliver, and it's all fun and meaningful, but the product is never my show. It is my client's show.

Could I conceive of stopping the thing, the very thing, that makes what I do extraordinary? Wouldn't that be like a doctor saying *"I know you came here because you want to be healthy, but today we are working on my own health"*?

Do I have the courage to focus on work I want to do, as opposed to focusing on good works others want me to do? I don't know how to do that, yet.

<u>John</u>: I want to stop the hesitation to act. The second-guessing. The pursuit of perfection. All of this is a dance of wandering, wiggling, and wavering on decisions, an unnecessary dance because in fact, I already know what I need to do.

For my life to fully go, I have to surrender to that knowledge. I need to stop the hesitation dance.

And now's your turn: **What needs to stop for my life
to really go?**

Do I love what I have?

<u>John</u>: It would be good to at least understand the material things I possess. It's crazy to open a drawer of T-shirts, look in the closet or some storage space, and find things that I wasn't even aware that I own. This speaks volumes to the ephemeral nature of human satisfaction, which I felt when, a while back, I actually bought this tangible thing I don't even remember having.

Moving from material to immaterial possessions, I don't fully know what's inside of me. What I'm good at. What skills, competencies, and talents I have. I've been given a lot more than I will ever know.

I have so much, perhaps too much.

Today I am forcing myself to love the process of discovering what I have, what I can offer, how I can contribute. And I'm trying to appreciate the freedom and opportunity to even consider the question of what I have.

<u>Olympia, 8 years old</u>: I love my mom and dad. But I wouldn't say 'no' to a puppy. *

<u>Cristina</u>: I absolutely love what I have. Otherwise, why have it?

At this point of my existence, I have invested a tremendous amount of discipline, thought, and resources into making sure that everything I have is something I love. And by that, I am speaking about as broadly as one could. The body, the family, all material possessions, friendships, work plus the people I work with, values, beliefs, stories, even goals for the future and memories of the past; I love my all. My face, my thoughts, my words, my deeds. The last sock, pair of underwear, spoon, or napkin. ***Every. Single. Thing.***

Each is measured, decided upon, and selected. If it's not loved, it goes, or better yet, never comes in. Life is too precious to have in our life things we do not love.

But.

And yes, this is a big "but" - there's always a difference between loving what I have, and thinking that what I have, no matter how loved, is enough. And of course, the kicker here is that "enough" is subject to a different set of questions because however saccharine the idea of love conquering all might seem, love is seldom enough on its own.

And now's your turn: **Do I love what I have?**

261

If I had one opportunity to time travel, where would I go?

<u>Jayden, 9 years old</u>: I would go 100 years before the end of the world to see flying cars.

<u>Emery, 17 years old:</u> The American Revolution. To see what the founding fathers were actually thinking and talking about, to understand their "why".

This is a very important moment in history. As I see it, a door was opened for the potential of a more perfect union and the development of a new model for how countries could be more just. A model of how a given government is going to serve the people.

I always wonder how completely the Founding Fathers actually believed that.

<u>Andrea, 16 years old:</u> I would go back to middle school before COVID. I want to see what normal was again and what happened. Back then I was a kid and nothing mattered. Something in me matured. After the pandemic, I became more aware that I am growing up.

<u>Cristina:</u> To my daughter's 65th birthday party. I would like to take her and her children on a trip around the world, to be together, to hug, kiss, and say sweet things to each other. To see her. To see her family, my descendants.

I just bawled my eyes out writing this. Yep. Good destination.

<u>McKenzie, 16 years old:</u> Definitely to the past, not the future. I don't know what's going to happen and I want to experience it for myself.

John: I have so many unanswered questions about the past, my ancestors. But that has already happened, and I am now here, therefore I am drawn to the future. Not because of the future being my legacy, but to see what happened to my dreams and fears.

I would go to the future, three generations from now, to walk amongst those not born yet, and learn about their dreams, bathing in the reality of a new world of assumptions and ideas. Not to find out whether we were wrong or right, but to admire the unimaginable ambitions of the world ahead.

And now's your turn: **If I had one opportunity to time travel, where would I go?**

Where do my thoughts come from?

<u>Evelyn, 13 years old</u>: They come from my heart and my emotions. They are instinctual. I am trying to think more logically. But I am a very sensitive and emotional person.

<u>Cristina</u>: I am a *Creator*, a demiurge. Not in the digital media understanding of the word, but of the divine kind.

As such, I am the universe made manifest in human form, just like you are, too. This is in our nature, because in order to exist, gravity needs something to exercise its pull and push on, and thus, my thoughts are the transmission medium for everything. Esoteric? Yes. Validated by math? Most certainly.

My thoughts are the product of neurons firing, electrical impulses in their most basic form. My thoughts are energy, and as such they come from where everything comes - the quantum. Thoughts are convergences because we are the vehicles for entropy.

We are tools and gods, and our thoughts are tools and gods.

<u>John</u>: When I was very young, I believed I came up with my own thoughts. I came to realize there is an extraordinary Slide Master of ideas surfacing in microseconds, ideas that haunted and inspired me, ideas about something that happened or could happen, remarkably new and different.

I've come to learn that thoughts come from a confluence of connections and interconnections of a neural tapestry woven of DNA threads and chromosomal stitches from 1000s of years ago. Truths of the present, regrets of the past, fears of the future, the light, the heat, the temperature of the body, the state of emotions, all conspire to push that Slide Master faster and differently.

265

My thoughts are part of the commons of human consciousness.

I am not my thoughts, and those thoughts are just as interesting as the clouds in the sky, hence I am more like the sky. Thoughts pass, because they always do. And the sky is always there.

And now's your turn: **Where do my thoughts come from?**

Why am I in a rush?

<u>Cristina</u>: I am in a rush because life is short. Also, because I am an idiot.

But seriously, I am in a rush because I am mortal. Because I am conditioned to believe that rushing is some stupid badge of virtue (which it is not). Because (Newtonian) time waits for no one. Because life is so nuanced, variegated, rich with possibilities and paths to explore, that the only elusive and possibly ineffective way to embrace it is to (sometimes), hurry the fuck up. Because most people just yearn, or talk, or dream, or wish for certain things they could be pursuing. I do these things (the yearning, talking or dreaming), and that, more often than not, requires some operational urgency that cannot be helped.

Rushing doesn't feel good though, and it also doesn't look good, because rushing kills excellence and the creation of spectacular details; and I am all about spectacular details. Rushing is also kinda naïve, especially when disconnected from what's actually required.

Most of us are in a rush because of a baseline addiction to our own stress chemistry.

I am getting better at it though… Now excuse me while I go make myself a cup of tea.

<u>John</u>: I once heard the great basketball coach John Wooden urge us all to *"be quick but don't hurry."* I love that.

We are all speed demons. We like to see things happen faster, whether it's immediate gratification or something that needs to change, something selfish or a form of justice. We want everything sooner. Time seems to be our enemy.

Waiting is challenging. We have lower and lower tolerances for impatience, frustration, and inaction, and this contributes to our irrational rush, especially in our modern context of material abundance and near infinite choices. But frustration and patience, if we let them, could become our greatest teachers.

Whatever it is, we all want it immediately, at a good price, and of high quality, but these attributes exist in a dynamic tension. During my corporate days, my first marketing director once said *"Speed, price, quality - pick two."* I always wanted speed; that was a given. And then I was always tortured by having to decide between price and quality. Was I willing to pay for the rush and the quality, or was I more price conscious? Such is life. There is an illusion we could get all three at once; not true.

We can be quick, but we can't rush, or we will miss too much. Regrets are made from rushing and missing what is really important.

And now's your turn: **Why am I in a rush?**

How are my successes and failures intertwined?

<u>Luca, 15 years old</u>: My successes and failures are on the same path. I experience failure and success as part of a unified story.

<u>Cristina</u>: These two things are frenemies with blurry delineations. What might feel like a failure today, could look different six months later. Past a certain point, the higher the number of tactical "failures" one can withstand, the higher the level of "success" one might experience. We are each the sum of everything that we have done, and all of it is additive. Last year's failures have fueled this year's success and so on… It's simple.

I do not focus at all on these labels. Or who knows, maybe I am eschewing definitions because I am still trying to understand what success actually means.

<u>John</u>: Success and failure are two sides of the same coin. The light and the shadow. Everything is connected in the waves of the world. The crests and the troughs, the apex and the nadir. We can't have one without the other. All income has its costs. All victories have their losses. They are tied together.

We may think that successes are the most important, the most valuable. But if we are interested in learning and becoming better, then we have to savor the failures. However cliché this might be, we need to be failing forward. And we need faster failures. If we are to truly grow into what we might be, we have to take chances.

And now's your turn: **How are my successes and failures intertwined?**

Over whom do I feel superior?

<u>Luca, 15 years old</u>: I feel superior over past versions of myself.

<u>Tanya, 12 years old</u>: I feel superior over people with no self-confidence because if you don't believe in yourself, you can't really do much until you acquire a little bit of confidence. I feel I can do more than someone with no self-confidence.

<u>John:</u> Feeling superior was one of the step ladders in my egotistical ascendancy to believe myself better, smarter, more capable than other people. There was a time when I felt superior over almost everybody, holding material success as the hollow marker. It helped me survive, but I paid a high price for this mindset, and temporarily diminished my humanity. By looking down, I missed the breadth and depth of wisdom I could have experienced from everyone around me.

Today, I question superiority as a concept. I question the concept of status, the rigged scales of meritocracy, and the game of Darwinian capitalism. I dismantled my ladder. I strive to be humbled by the unknown.

<u>Cristina</u>: Most everyone, isn't that obvious?

Absurdity aside, feelings of superiority, when they do occur, are episodes of my stupidity, because the universe is incredibly hilarious and stupendously adroit at immediately cutting me to size when I get too cocky. And because I don't like how that divine sense of humor feels on bare skin as the adjustment hits, I literally scrub the toilets in my house on a regular basis to remind myself to stay humble, while in parallel, continuously keeping an eye on the karma balance sheet. A practice which I wholeheartedly endorse.

I Triple Dog Dare you to feel superior while scrubbing toilets.

And now's your turn: **Over whom do I feel superior?**

To whom do I feel inferior?

<u>Tanya, 12 years old</u>: This is a hard question, but I am thinking of my mother. Because she IS my mother. Also, because she puts boundaries in my life. My mother literally birthed me, and that's a lot. It's not 100% accurate to say that I am feeling inferior to her, but my parents do have more knowledge, and they are also taller. I am not feeling inferior to them by very much, but a little, yes. That makes sense to me.

<u>Luca, 15 years old</u>: I usually feel inferior to the people I learn from because they know more. And yes, I can take advice from my peers, and in general, I can take advice from people to whom I do not feel inferior, but I might not pay as much attention to them if I perceive them as my equals.

<u>John</u>: The perpetually downward elevator of inferiority is always at the ready. With awareness, I can use it to connect to what is real. But most often, this sense of inferiority puts a bad thought in my mind, and pulls me down.

I have spent a lot of time telling myself that I am deserving of what I have. That I'm not faking it. I work hard to escape the imprisonment of inadequacy. And yet, to be knocked off my little pedestal of courage, is an act which is easily done. Most of the time I do it to myself: I meet someone, I see someone, I witness someone doing something that I think I should do, could do, should have done, and that triggers regrets and second guessing of how I've lived.

I have learned to avoid this dreadful elevator. But it is easy to be pushed through the shaft, and crash in the basement of inferiority.

The floor of confidence is fragile.

<u>Cristina</u>: Amongst a zillion things I could name which would illustrate my unquestionable inferiority, I already know that I am incapable of juggling three objects, and that my basketball dunking is abysmal. But to give thought to such shortcomings would be akin to feeling inferior to the speed of a cheetah. That stuff just is.

Feeling inferior to a given person or group of humans is a waste of time and a waste of the potential I do carry within. Because of the absolute relativity of such a concept, I choose to feel inferior to nobody.

Yes, cheetahs exist and they are faster than me. Yes, there are, have been, and will always be people that are luckier, richer, more beautiful, smarter, better, and more accomplished than I could ever be. That's a fact.

While I am worse than many on a dizzying spectrum of dimensions, I choose to never give someone the power to make me feel inferior. Inferiority is an artificial construct without any objective evaluation system, a state which at best depletes us of the juices of life, and at worst cripples us. I'll have none of that, and I encourage you too to do the same.

I am awesome.

You are awesome.

We are awesome.

Now, as I said, let's go scrub some more toilets.

And now's your turn: **To whom do I feel inferior?**

277

Should I feel guilty about my privilege?

<u>Luca, 15 years old</u>: Intelligence and beauty are tickets to a warehouse of privileges. People believe you. I have these things, and I shouldn't feel guilty about it.

<u>Tanya, 12 years old</u>: I have a lot of privilege. Most definitely!

I have a very good life; I travel a lot and my friends are great. Also, I am beautiful and quite intelligent, I am physically strong and artistically talented, so all this amounts to a lot of privilege. I am not sure if I should feel guilty about it, but definitely I should feel grateful. My parents work hard to give me all I have, to give me this life.

But feeling guilty? Why would I do that? It's not like I rip money out of people's hands or anything!

<u>Cristina</u>: Always and never, while perpetually walking this fine line with dignity and a meaningful contribution to the rest of the world, especially for those who don't have what I have. My personal history with a childhood deprived of both human rights and basic necessities, only layers complexity atop my current privilege.

Now, if it is to split hairs, I do acknowledge that there are many types of privilege, some over which a person has no control (like skin color or some other birth-given attribute), some over which a person has control (like money or status), and some which have been earned through great toil and sacrifice (my American citizenship comes to mind, although the list is long).

What purpose could be served by feeling guilty about my skin color? I can be grateful, and I can behave in a way that makes me an ally, not a perpetrator of silence and deed. Guilt would serve no useful purpose. For privileges I have worked a lifetime to achieve (chiefly professional), the only culpability I feel is doing too little, too slow.

Material and consumer privileges are very tricky, and here's where guilt does its dance. I have lucid nightmares about most goods I purchase: what slavery might they fuel? What raping of the earth might that be? How is this fair to my grandmother who never had a washing machine - and the millions of women like her who are washing, for the hundredth time - the same shirt in the same polluted river? Etcetera. Buying things is fraught with deeply uncomfortable emotions. Above all else though, guilt is an ugly, energy-wasting effort I find neither virtuous nor desirable because guilt confers no badge of absolution on the person feeling it.

Religions are quick to tell us what we should and shouldn't feel guilty about - to the naked eye, more of a control mechanism, than atonement tool. Perhaps the best we could do is to be mindful, to tread lightly, to use whatever we have (from health to water, money, and power) with gentle, loving, kindness towards everything and everyone. It's way simpler than guilt, no?

John: Guilt is a waste of time. Let's just pile our plates full of awareness, teaching, and learning. With a heaping serving of gratitude. Not guilt.

Privilege is fuel. Privilege is a source of energy. Privilege is having a head start.

Making sure that I avoid the indigestion of another serving of guilt, I want to just take advantage of the privilege I have to simply accelerate myself and help others.

And now's your turn: **Should I feel guilty about my privilege?**

What do I trust?

<u>Emery, 17 years old</u>: I trust logic. I'm not necessarily trusting the ideas that people have, but the concept of logic itself. I trust the process of logic where you can deduce a set of facts, and then extrapolate things. I trust that if we do use logic properly, we can achieve good results. The mechanism of logic itself has no flaws. That's the thing I trust the most.

<u>John</u>: I've really made it a personal objective to trust everybody. More often than not, I have been rewarded. And yes, I've also been burned at times, but I've tried not to become callous or wary of the potential to have that universal trust fulfilled. It's easy to say *"The last time I did this it didn't work out"* and forget that today, the circumstances are not the same. My default is trusting that there is good in everything and everyone.

<u>Cristina</u>: This is not a particularly precise line of inquiry and I grew up in a paranoid totalitarian society, so I might need a qualifier first, such as, *"trust with what?"*

With milk money, I trust everyone.

With my life, I trust my husband, my daughter, and a select few.

With nuclear weapons… I trust the mechanics that maintain the silos we were idiotic enough to build.

In general, I think most people are honest if given the chance, and on a daily basis, I adopt the healthy practice of not tempting people out of their honesty. Let's incentivize good behaviors!

Above all however, I trust myself because I have a good track record, and when it comes to trust, evidence is key.

And now's your turn: **What do I trust?**

What is something I couldn't live without?

<u>Cristina</u>: Stories in book form.

<u>Sofia, 16 years old</u>: I couldn't live without dance. It's how I express myself and how I connect with the world on a deeper level. *

<u>John</u>: The one thing I want to preserve, the one thing I would like until the end of my days, is freedom. Freedom to be and to think, freedom to enjoy whatever I have, material, relational, and sensual.

And now's your turn: **What is something I couldn't live without?**

Am I a good friend?

<u>Luca, 15 years old</u>: I think I am a good friend, but definitely not to everyone. I am a very good friend to my besties, but to those I just casually know, I don't feel the fuel of connection, so we don't talk much. Being a good friend is to care about the other, plus to stay in touch. If you don't, it doesn't matter if you move a mountain on occasion for that person; you're still not a good friend.

<u>Cristina</u>: A bit of a righteous jerk with an oversized soapbox and a set of too-high expectations, but in essence, yes, I am a spectacular friend that absolutely would build a raft out of empty soda bottles and then immediately paddle across the Pacific using nothing but my bare hands, just so I could rescue your stranded ass.

"Friend" is a word that gets tossed around a lot. And it should be, perhaps, a singularly special word for a special human, a human that transcends our journey through jobs, serial romances, or money tribulations.

Being a good friend is a commitment to inconvenience myself on behalf of someone else's wellbeing, and being glad of it. Being a good friend is transcending tiredness, and most definitely, transcending busyness. Being a good friend is staying in touch. Listening. Doing. Holding the discomfort of hard things being said, even when not knowing what to do or say about it. Not running away.

Being a good friend is showing up, warts and all, truth and all, over, and over, and over again. It's pretty simple, actually.

<u>John</u>: I just want to be able to say "yes" to this question. I know my intentions are good, which is meaningless. And I always try to be a good friend – more meaninglessness.

I know what a good friend is. The unconditional, the empathetic and compassionate support you feel from someone. And I aspire to that.

But my bluntness can get me into trouble. While good friends need to be truth tellers, sometimes I do let my interests and my desire to control take some of the good out of my friendships.

Nevertheless, this is a battle I might be actually winning, because I am working hard to focus on understanding my friends. To listen more. To be in their shoes. To simply be ready to give them what they need, when they need it.

And now's your turn: **Am I a good friend?**

287

How do I feel about my body?

<u>Thalia,12 years old:</u> While I am definitely not the most physical person, I am working on that. I think I will never say *"Wow, I have the most perfect, amazing shape!"* It is hard, but if I am thinking of my body in terms of what it can do, my body is a good dancer, it can play soccer, its vocal cords can sing. That's how I see it: more about what I do than how I look.

<u>Cristina</u>: I am a woman, OK?

Which means I am asking myself this question about 300 times a day, possibly even in my sleep, because I have been conditioned since birth to question its worth for reasons that often have nothing to do with my body at all. On the daily, my female form becomes the recurring, mundane battleground and scapegoat conduit in the peddling of some snake oil or another - consumer goods, religion, legislation, politics, and social norms included. And if this sentence makes no sense to you, you are probably not a woman.

What I am TRYING to feel about my body is something a bit different.

During the rare instance when I manage to forget all the societal, global, hyper-local, cultural, traditional and non-traditional, gendered, sexual, romantic, iconic, dogmatic and economic frameworks heaped upon that part of my body called "shoulders", the core feeling is gratefulness laced with a certain sense of inadequate behavior that could do justice to the magnificent vessel I have been gifted at birth, if only...

There's so much potential in the human body, and much of it I have been given - from fast-twitch muscles, to beauty, intelligence, health, and so on. I don't feel that I give such gifts justice in all the ways my body deserves.

What I want is to have nothing but love, delight, and gratitude towards my body. Nothing else is ever required, for the simple reason that we exist.

<u>John</u>: I remember when I was younger and I asked my barber what he thought I should do about my hair loss. He said: *"Like what?"* I shrugged. He grabbed my face as he looked at me in the mirror and said, *"I never thought your hair defined you."* He is the philosopher-stylist who got a big tip that day.

We can improve our looks, but we are who we are.

I want to believe in the *wabi sabi* of life, the beautiful Japanese philosophy that values deterioration as equally beautiful as youthfulness. It's not an easy concept.

Today, I believe that wrinkles are signs of experience, the rings of my tree. That gray hair does communicate lived wisdom. That my fat pockets are proof that I have enjoyed whatever I drank and ate. This visible record that my body represents is memorabilia I've collected, a chart of what I have been given, what I've taken, and what I've accomplished.

I made peace with my body.

And now's your turn: **How do I feel about my body?**

Who is the foreigner?

<u>John</u>: In our delusions, the foreigner is the person who is alien to us; the people which are not supposed to be "here".

While squarely American by birth, I've always been a foreigner. I have been perpetually trying to assimilate and feel fully assimilated, emigrating into the world of full acceptance. I have been constantly fighting to be what others want me to be, against what I'm trying to become. This struggle to cross the border into authenticity, and this rejection, has made me a foreigner my entire life.

<u>Audrey, 15 years old</u>: I am a foreigner so maybe I am also THE foreigner.

<u>Cristina</u>: Nobody is a foreigner. There are no "others". Everyone is "us".

Not because it is easy to include everyone (it is not). Not because I understand or relate to everyone (I don't). Not because I feel I belong (while I know that we all technically belong, I feel excluded from activities, opportunities, groups, and cultures with painful and disturbing periodicity). Not because my needs are met (they are not). Not because I am objective (most days I am hair-trigger angry and incendiary as a fed-up banshee).

But because I made the decision a decade ago that I work for 10 billion people, including those not born yet, including those I don't like, respect, or trust (and yes, we all feel that there are people in the world which we do not like, respect, or trust). And once you work for someone, then the game changes: you can't really be much of an a-hole towards your employers. So yeah, nobody is really a foreigner.

When my fears and prejudices try to raise their heads, I observe it, cringe, and then release it, reminding myself that *"this person is my boss"*. You're either a servant leader, or doing lip service, and lip service has never been my style.

And now's your turn: **Who is the foreigner?**

Is it true when I say that "I don't have time"?

<u>Evelyn, 13 years old</u>: Most of the time that's not true. I have a lot of free time I waste. If I say that, it's an emotional reaction. When in reality I do have free time.

<u>Cristina</u>: Unless one is on death's doorstep, no. There is always time for the things that are truly relevant to us.

While energy levels, temperament, life philosophy, and skill-sets vary widely between people, this conglomerate of traits influences how one deals with the nature of time. For example, I hold the quirky belief that everyone can close their eyes and draw time from the quantum which makes me both acutely aware of time's dimension, and rarely worried about it.

<u>John</u>: The truth is irrelevant because the feeling is real: someone has hijacked our available time. We have a complaint and we want answers from the Time Allocation Department! We got short-changed. Someone told us there were 24 hours in a day and it feels like 24 minutes!

Seneca said 2000 years ago, *"It is not that we have a short span of time, but that we waste much of it. Life is long enough, and it has been given in sufficiently generous measure to allow the accomplishment of the very greatest things if the whole of it is well invested."*.

What is at the top of our to do list? The easy stuff? The stuff we have to do? Or the stuff we want to do?

We have too many interests and dreams. Too many options. Too many excuses when choosing what's most important, relevant and meaningful. The equation of how finite our time is, with a coefficient of prioritization, and the vector of action, should beg us to pay fierce attention to what we actually do, and then we'll have more time.

And now's your turn: **Is it true when I say that "I don't have time"?**

Winter

What is Winter?

Darkness. Dormancy. Reparation.

Pleasure that emerges from the pain.

What is holding me back from my dreams?

<u>Emery, 17 years old</u>: Hesitance and fear. Fear of the unknown. Fear of taking risks. Fear of self-sabotage, fear that I would be doing something wrong, some unexpected action against my own dreams.

<u>Cristina:</u> There's only one answer to that for all of us: ourselves. Yes, it's a trick question with a forever-in-your-face glaring answer, because the only thing that CAN hold us back is us.

The point is this: we have to discover what narratives, fears, and heritage bullshit holds us back. In absence of that, we have to ignore that baggage altogether. Either way, we have to consciously choose to move past it.

We have to head where we want to go regardless of the showtunes riffing inside. The psychoanalytic excavation is entirely optional, and often a detour done on purpose. As a former recipient of 500+ hours of therapy, I can attest that it is both fascinating and useful, but it has to be done IN PARALLEL with whatever else needs doing.

I choose to hide behind nothing. If an action I am contemplating scares the crap out of me, it's a safe bet that I probably should do it, and no, I don't mean bungee-jumping, although maybe that too has its place.

So yeah. I know that I am always the most dangerous and persistent enemy I could ever have, and I need to be on the lookout for subversive treachery this enemy might be inflicting at the least opportune moment. And by "me" I mean "you".

<u>John:</u> As I get more reflective, I realize that my selfish imaginings of what I wanted were nothing but self-absorbed, micro-yearnings. Slowly, my dreams made way for a bigger set of targets.

Maybe it is age, maybe it is my grasping at a legacy and my children's futures, but my capacity to dream has grown into a radically exponential vision of supporting other people's dreams. I want to enable others; to be freed from a self-centered focus and to tune into the joy of being part of a broader constellation.

The biggest obstacle has always been me, the single ego which separates and segregates us, fractionalizing *our* dreams.

"Me" impedes the greatest dream of "We".

And now's your turn: **What is holding me back from my dreams?**

What is my biggest regret so far?

<u>Lily, 15 years old</u>: I am a very regretful person. I'm indecisive. Indecision and regret go hand in hand. If you make the wrong decision, then you feel regret. I don't really know if I have a big regret, because I feel regret so often. And in a few weeks, or a few months, or a year later, it doesn't matter anymore.

<u>Cristina</u>: My biggest regret is believing that my dad was immortal. He wasn't, and I wasted time we could have spent together - a lesson I would have rather not had to learn the hard way. So please, let's spend more time with those we love! As much time as we can. Better yet, more time than we think we have available. We'll probably be glad we did.

<u>Tanya, 12 years old</u>: When I was six or seven, I let myself be influenced by a friend and I lied to people.

<u>John</u>: I used to pride myself in saying *No Regrets!* It was catchy and people liked it. I was trying to tell myself to be conscious of the present. Not to be hedonistic, but to be ready for the unexpected. With this motto, I was opening doors for my career and life.

Today I define as "regrets" mostly the things that I did not do, and not so much the mistakes that I made. While those form memories I don't like, what I regret the most is not taking the opportunities that I could have, opportunities which might have transformed me into the best version of myself. I could have been more authentic, more compassionate, more loving. I could have really listened. I could have put other people before my own needs.

These regrets are vivid and palpable lessons that could have pushed me out of selfishness and into selflessness - an extraordinary curriculum for personal evolution.

I do not dwell on it. These things are done and history! Some still make me cringe. Some make me smile, because I know I'm better today. But I forbid myself the indulgence of dwelling on my regrets because they can become small tumors that grow, weigh us down, and metastasize

I make sure that I am not a regret collector. The few I do have, are part of who I am, and not swept under the carpet. Benign regrets are illuminating reminders of how far I have traveled on the path that continues to stretch forward.

And now's your turn: **What is my biggest regret so far?**

When is enough, enough?

<u>Lily, 15 years old</u>: You could have all the money in the world, a great job, and a great family, but if it was just given to you and you didn't earn it yourself, I think you won't feel truly satisfied. For me, it is about working hard and earning things. I want to be feeling proud of myself, and happy with what I've accomplished. That would be enough.

<u>John</u>: In 1997 I was the founding CEO of an online education company. Like most startups, we used stock options as the incentive to elicit the blood, sweat, and tears that were necessary to build a company that might have a chance at an exit.

My first hire was a guy named Victor, a Vietnamese-born Chinese young man who escaped with his family as refugees, just as the Vietnam war was ending. It's a classic American Dream story. Victor learned the language and fully integrated into American culture. He went to college and did extremely well. He was an entrepreneurial athlete. In startups, because you don't know exactly who you need, you need people who are like Swiss Army knives. And Victor was one of such humans.

Jack was another one of my young employees, equally talented and hungry. As young employees often do, Victor and Jack started to talk about their dreams, about what will happen when their stock options become real, and they become millionaires. Jack was detailing the type of car he would buy, the type of watch he would purchase, luxuries that he could not yet afford.

Victor replied: *"I don't need those things. My dad has suffered a lot to get to this country. He's sick. He's given me everything. And he has this silly, crazy dream that he wants to drive a Mercedes as the symbol of our family's success in this country. And while I know it's not the true symbol, I'm going to buy him his Mercedes. If I have any money left, I'm going to pay off the mortgage on their home because I don't want them to worry about money anymore."*

Victor was not trying to one-up anybody. He was just speaking from the heart, fulfilling a different kind of dream.

I'm often reminded of that conversation as an exercise to focus on what is important. What do I need? What is enough? What could we do for others if we had a little more? For many of us, when we hear the word "enough" we think of material things, we think of money. We don't think of love. We think of things that revolve around our ego.

We are afflicted by a global epidemic of "more", "better", and "never enough", but the truth is that "enough" should be the end. Otherwise "not enough" is the beginning of way too much.

Victor's dad drove a Mercedes until he died.

<u>Cristina</u>: One day, I was on a bus to the ruins of Machu Picchu, and I found myself crying like a baby because at that very moment, the life I imagined decades before when I was a hungry kid had exceeded all my expectations. Like a Magellan-era explorer, I was at the known edge of the map. And that was before reaching the ruins! I immediately decided that everything which would come afterwards is a bonus, and that from this moment on, I could never complain that something is not enough.

In hindsight, Machu Picchu was also a rather modest benchmark showing me that <u>we dream too small and don't know how to want</u>. Read that again please.

Enough is absolutely enough when we can actually restrain ourselves from contemplating our bank accounts just to buy another pair of shoes, or from ogling the buffet to get a fifth helping of cake - which I have been known to do on occasion. That's the only dimension where we need to hold the concept of "enough" at eye level. Enough gluttony, enough consumerism, enough petty power, or fat on the gut.

Beyond that, nothing is ever enough because we have been accidentally designed as the vanguards of life: to perpetually learn, to constantly push the boundaries of our existence, to seek, to be curious. This is Homo Sapiens' mission as a species.

I don't want to ever run my fingers against the far edge of love, or the bottom drawer of knowledge. My roving of this Newtonian space will only be ended by the terminus point of my days - and before then, there is never enough.

Enough is never enough because we're mortal.

And now's your turn: **When is enough, enough?**

What am I afraid of?

<u>Lily, 15 years old</u>: Probably bugs all over me. But my actual worst fear is that we are all in a simulation and it glitches, and then I'm stuck in a void for eternity. And I don't die, so I'm just there, with no one to talk to, and nothing to do. That would be the worst possible scenario: to be alone forever.

<u>John</u>: Fear comes in many forms. I had very close friends who were having their first baby, and the mother had nightmares that her son was going to be born with six fingers and six toes on each foot and hand. Six fingers! She kept talking about it. She was obsessed. So, when this young man was born, the father rushed to the side of the mother and cuddled the baby. *"Count the toes!"* she urged. And he counted: *"1, 2, 3, 4, 5 ...6"*. And then again: *"1, 2, 3, 4, 5, and... 6"*. There were indeed 12 fingers and 12 toes! The sixth finger and toe were boneless pieces of skin but they looked like fingers and toes. Her fear came true. Yet, ultimately, it had no bearing on the wellbeing of the child who today is a very accomplished guitarist. We can be right about our fears and wrong about the consequences.

<u>Cristina</u>: I fear the smallness that fear brings to my life much more than the fear itself.

Every day, I choose to live with as little fear as possible. Fearlessness is a practice. It's an energetic place of honor which I aim to inhabit over, and over, and over again despite the terror I might feel in a given human moment. It's a value. It's almost a sin - and I love the sinfulness of it. This is not theory, it's a lived experience.

Being fearless: nothing else feels like it. Fearlessness can be a lifestyle, and I think it is worth the price one has to pay for it.

And now's your turn: **What am I afraid of?**

What will my legacy be?

<u>Luca, 15 years old</u>: A home, pictures of me from when I was younger, maybe some awards and public recognition of sorts, a bit of wealth for my children to have… I think that would be good. Let's not be too greedy.

<u>John</u>: Fame is fleeting and over-rated. Being remembered well past one's life is pure ego.

There is this granular energy within us and when we are truthful and sincere in what we do, what we say ripples forward and backward, igniting a thought, an idea, a caring action in someone else's mind. Yes, what we do can inspire and motivate, but it is subtle and mysterious. People constantly acquire little things from others, and those become part of the beautiful commons of our shared space.

Love is the greatest legacy. Did we wholeheartedly love our opportunity, our community, and the living species around us?

Our legacies are a string of microscopic moments that can profoundly influence the future in which no one will remember us. And that's how it should be.

<u>Cristina</u>: My legacy should be an echo that reverberates in souls, and in the winds of the world, long beyond my heartbeat. And I hope for 100,000 years of survival for our global society as a result of each of our actions. Having names ascribed to a footnote of history is thoroughly optional.

While I know I have already changed lives, a true legacy goes beyond that.

I have loved deeply. I have given, profoundly. I have walked, again and again, to the edge of that thing that was there for me to explore.

I have seen, I have felt, I have lived. I will continue to do so, given the chance.

It has to be enough in the end.

And now's your turn: **What will my legacy be?**

Is this all there is?

<u>John</u>: Yes. This moment that we're sharing right now, is all we can really count on. And while we have designs on where the path should lead, could lead, might lead, this is all we get. This little brief interlude between what is past and what is future.

But maybe you're thinking about this question differently. Maybe you're 19, 39, 59 years old. And you're wondering if this path ahead is all there is, with your commitments, obligations, investments, burdens, and bills to pay that lock you down to a very definitive and rather limiting space and time. And if that's the case, before you cry for clarification, I am here to say that no, this is not all there is, and there can be more, much more, to life.

To get there, you might require an exercise in disillusionment, which means an effort to remove the illusion. Maybe you think that you're too old, or that's too late, maybe you think there's nothing you can do.

All illusions. These are the signs that you've lost your mojo, that someone might be robbing you of your agency, or that the moment to make a change is here. I am here to tell you that yes, there are many risks and dangers for switching horses in the middle of the ride but that's up to you. You could quit your job, change your relationships, move somewhere new. At any point of our lives, we can design a new identity no matter our stage and age.

<u>Lily, 15 years old</u>: The world is not going to change unless you try to change it. Other people will change it for you, but your world is not going to change. If you're unhappy with where you are, you should do something about that. You shouldn't just expect it to adjust for you on its own accord.

<u>Cristina</u>: Are you still breathing? If yes, then no, this is not all there is.

When at any point I find myself despondent, or wanting more, I need to give that "more" to others first, because the more I give, the more I get. It never fails. A bit counterintuitive, I know.

Do I want more money? Then I should first be more generous with my money.

Do I want more love? Then I should first give more affection to others while allowing myself to feel the love already swirling invisible around me.

Do I want more understanding? Then I should first listen more.

Do I want more prestige, more career advancement, etc.? Then I should help others achieve theirs.

And so on.

There's no substitute in life for the atomic power of walking towards those things we want by giving them first to others.

Let's not waste time asking if this is all there is. The question itself points to dark territories of ungrateful shadows and entitlement. Even more dangerously, it points to unlit corridors of depression and hopelessness.

Let's avoid it at all costs. Let's explore, push (inwards and outwards), and revel in the magnificence of aliveness, because everything that exists, exists to be shared.

And be careful; this issue can, literally, kill you.

And now's your turn: **Is this all there is?**

What if I am wrong?

<u>John</u>: I might be wrong about everything.

We rely on assumptions that lead to inaccurate conclusions exposing the simplistic notion that a single frame from the film of life would tell us what the film is about. While the story keeps going like a bad Tarzan movie where we grab a vine and then keep swinging through the jungle, we are so focused on our vines, on our points of view, that we can never fully understand what is going on in the whole jungle. We just want something solid to hold on to, and that tiny useful part of the ecosystem, that perspective we embrace, becomes the complete jungle to us.

Trying to be right (or more importantly perhaps, trying not to be wrong) is like trying to grab and hold water. It is virtually impossible. We put our small piece of rightness into a bucket, examine it, then make some specific observations, and perhaps, in the end, maybe we know water, even though life, relationships, and time are more like the river, the ocean, and the rainfall. In the end, even knowing water doesn't mean much.

I force myself to question my entire set of assumptions and beliefs, because being open to reality is more satisfying than being right.

<u>Cristina</u>: Being wrong is training, because it is statistically impossible to be right all the time. As annoying as it feels, learning that I am wrong is a set of markers to prevent drift.

One marker is for humbleness: I am swiftly cut to size when my conceptual idols fall off their pedestal, proven incorrect, miscalculated, or fully out-to-lunch. On occasion, I additionally learn if my humility is contrived, like when attempting to get bitter medicine down someone's throat and I say the words *"I might be wrong"*, even though I don't believe it. Gag!

The other marker is for progress, and I love being proven wrong on such occasions because feedback gives a new viewpoint and a gateway into new solutions.

When I am right but nonetheless stuck without the results I want, it's difficult; where do I go from there? But if I am mistaken, I actually get a lever for growth, fix the wrongness, and ta-da!

Either way, not being right either pushes me to become more human, enables me to help someone, or it's the kick in the pants necessary to get unstuck. Being wrong is fabulous!

And now's your turn: **What if I am wrong?**

What if my life is an illusion?

<u>John</u>: Of course life is an illusion!

When you really think about it, an illusion is an inaccurate reflection of reality. And humans have no real understanding of reality. If I step back and consider, science doesn't have a full picture yet of how our brain works, where our thoughts come from, what makes our genetic attributes good and bad, expressed or dormant.

We can falsely think there's some homunculus in our minds or in our skulls telling us what to do, even though, from a sensorial perspective, we cannot feel our thoughts. Even when we try to use 100% of our senses, everything we encounter gets filtered, shaped, focused or obliterated by our biases, DNA, life experiences and distractions.

We are able to capture only a tiny fraction of what's really happening around us, and our minds are constantly moving us away from what is real. The narratives we develop drive what we experience, so the way we perceive our lives, is a somewhat fictional movie loosely based on the truth.

Indeed, we are in an illusion. The question always is: can we pursue disenchantment? Can we make cracks in the false perceptions? Can we let the light of reality pierce through narratives, filters, and biases? The great imposition of what we think is there but actually does not exist is our biggest and thoroughly invisible enemy.

<u>Luca, 15 years old</u>: If my life is an illusion, then let's make it the best illusion anyway!

<u>Cristina</u>: In a dialectic sense, and, at a minimum, inside the quantum level, life IS an illusion.

Like a schizophrenic patient not knowing for sure what is real and what is not, I have been living for two decades as if nothing is real except myself, building mundane redundancies so I don't burn the house down or accidentally abandon the kid at the train station due to a misperception of reality.

Ultimately, we cannot know what is real (and yes, I am going pure-blood Platonian here). I choose this to mean that I possess full license to create my own reality. If we are in a holodeck, I might as well run a pleasant program of my own choosing.

Maybe we are simply experiencing sensations in the Matrix. And maybe we are not. Either way, let's savor the sun, the flowers, and the breeze, because perception is all there is anyway.

And now's your turn: **What if my life is an illusion?**

When will I apologize?

<u>Tanya, 12 years old</u>: I want to apologize to my mother for causing her pain when she birthed me. I want to apologize to the earth for what our species has done to it.

I also yelled some mean stuff, both unintentionally and intentionally, and I would like to say sorry for that. I have similarly said accidental things that caused sadness for others, and I would like to be able to apologize today.

<u>Cristina</u>: On his deathbed, my father really wanted to apologize to everyone. He even called the local priest to be his proxy.

Dad was always been kind and gentle, and I must have wondered out loud what was there for him to apologize, because he quickly gave me two examples: the harshness with which he felt he treated his students when he was a young teacher (particularly the boys), and the discrimination against *"the gypsies"* (i.e. the Roma community members living in his town). While Romanian society is heavily prejudiced against the Roma minority even today, he didn't feel that normalizing gave him a justification for past acts.

When I first read this question, I bristled: *"I don't have any reason to apologize!"* Which is proof why one should absolutely answer it.

First, I hereby apologize for being a bully in my childhood. I apologize for the blindness with which I walked through life the first couple of decades of my life, completely oblivious to the efforts my parents made during day-to-day life. I apologize for my teenage anger towards those much less equipped to withstand it, even if they were adults.

I apologize for being annoying on a regular basis. For using people. For periodically falling into the trap of entitlement and pride. For laziness. For not being there for others when I should have been. For being unnecessarily harsh even if I was right.

And while at it, I apologize for righteousness. For procrastination and impatience. For judging. For talking too much. For flaunting the things that were worth flaunting, even when hard earned. For making assumptions.

Above all, I apologize for loving too little when I could have opened my heart to so much more, for a systemic lack of compassion, for being less kind than I know I have it in me to be, and for being fearful when I should have been an example of courage.

This doesn't cover it all, I am certain, but it's a good start.

<u>Cash, 14 years old</u>: I'll apologize when I've messed up. I won't apologize for being myself or standing up for what I believe in.*

<u>John</u>: We are all in a 12 STEP program. While I've never been in AA, I have witnessed the effectiveness of its methodology, especially Step #9 *Make amends to those you've harmed.* This isn't meant to make us feel better—**its purpose is to sincerely apologize to others for the pain we've caused.**

Apologizing is woven with awareness and accountability for the harm I have done. This is not a one-time occurrence; it is a day-to-day, moment-to-moment experience during which my thoughts, actions, body language, lack of critical thinking, indiscretions and selfishness are causing various degrees of unintended and intended suffering.

What I could say is never enough. Amends need to be offered on a regular basis. I feel a deep need for a different way to live and think without harm, centered on kindness, keen awareness, and acknowledgement.

And now's your turn: **When will I apologize?**

What happens to me after death?

<u>John</u>: Worms.

Once our life force leaves the body, our physical manifestation is returned to dust through natural and inexorable processes. No matter what we looked like, how much money we made, whether we had two or four legs or wings, our energy is released back into the universe and reabsorbed by basic elements and sacred forces working to determine the destiny of the universe.

All our journeys end the same way.

<u>Andrea, 16 years old</u>: I honestly think our souls live on. Our bodies die and somehow our souls never leave.

<u>Cristina</u>: To quote Keanu Reeves, after we die, *the people who love us will miss us.*

Beyond that, we probably simply go to whence we came before we sparked to life in our mother's womb. It's just logical to look at being here as a mere stop on a larger, somewhat circular journey.

The body decays and nourishes the ecosystem, so, if you please, plant some spectacular flowers atop of me, rambling old pink roses that reach for the sky, and a weeping willow with curly branches, *Alliums* and *Fritillaria Imperialis* for spring blooms, some *Hellebores* to keep the party going during winter, *New Zealand Flax* for attitude because a girl needs swords even in death, and grasses - like *Stipa Gigantea* and *Calamagrostis x acutiflora 'Karl Foerster'* - to catch the wind and dance. I hope that whatever is mortal in me becomes this kind of life and beauty after death.

I believe my soul will linger for a while, watching above for the things I cared deeply about - peace comes to mind, and love, children, grandchildren, the work, the world. And then, when that is done, a next level will come, and I am excited too about that mystery.

And now's your turn: **What happens to me after death?**

How can I do less harm?

Emery, 17 years old: The main way I can do less harm is to pay attention to the emotional value of the present. I caused a lot of harm to myself by paying too much attention to the past and the future, forgetting to put an emotional value on the present.

The present is the only truth; the only reality. Past and future don't exist in the present. Once you get to the future, what we previously called "future" becomes "the present", and I might as well be there in the first place, because that's where life is.

John: Life is all about doing less harm.

I know it may sound like a catchphrase or a weak corporate credo, but everything we do, think, say, plus how we live, purchase and eat, has a component of harm in it. And we can make ourselves crazy. Without mentioning the nihilist fatalism invariably generated from such inquiry line, which often pushes us towards more individualistic, hedonistic, and selfish pursuits.

I have the opportunity to reduce the harm I do in all things. I have to consider the consequences of my actions, ideas, and thoughts.

I can do less harm by reminding myself that everything I do has a cost and an impact on others and the world.

Cristina: Intention, attention, connection. I don't know about you, but this is how I can do less harm.

Everything counts. Everything either harms or helps - our words, deeds, and choices have ramifications even when we can't see it.

Which is why it makes a difference if I strive to notice the invisible links between what I own, what I crave, what I mindlessly do, and how some of those things have consequences for people who are not me. It takes determination and some occasional paradigm shifts, but once I do that, I can live in less harmful ways, especially towards the environment.

I went to an event once and there was a huge poster asking: *"how many slaves worked for you today?"* A torturous question.

Who picked the fruits and vegetables in the fridge? Where do the coffee and roses come from? Who made the clothes on my back? What about the oil in the car? The electricity that powers it all? The civic peace and democracy I enjoy - what is its imperialist price? Where does the garbage go? What happens to my vote? Does it harm or help?

Intention, attention, connection. It seems to make a difference.

And now's your turn: **How can I do less harm?**

What are my self-sabotaging behaviors?

<u>Luca, 15 years old</u>: Adrenaline is a tricky thing and we have to be careful with it because it can lead to self-sabotage. Allowing stress to rule me is also a self-sabotaging behavior. Having a tape in my head saying *"I should do this, I need to do that, and I should do those other things too..."* and not doing actually anything about it, is, clearly, self-sabotage. I probably catch myself at it every day. If I know I should, then I might as well just do it and be done. I am working towards that.

<u>John</u>: Led by my inner perfectionist, I regularly get on the merry-go-round of self-sabotage. This carny carousel operator has a visceral need to re-edit something that is already done. It pushes me to fix something that is complete. This miscreant wants to make notes in the margins of a major speech mere seconds before I give it. And it often prevents the completion of tasks I need to deliver.

If there was unlimited time, I could make everything better, especially if I could stop the other evil force: procrastination. I use procrastination and perfection to power the nuclear engine of self-sabotage. By not giving myself enough time to prepare, while harboring a deep desire to be perfect, I create anxiety for myself and everybody around me.

I want to fully surrender to the completion of my work through awareness and presence; through appreciation for what has been done, and gratitude for the opportunity to do so. I hope that one day I can accept that creativity and expression are just points on an infinite continuum.

<u>Cristina</u>: I am not special in my self-sabotaging behaviors: I eat too much sugar, I don't watch my money as closely as I should, and I prioritize *"fun"* before *"important"* way too often. I don't know what to do to curb such behaviors, other than tediously

bending my will-power like a crowbar, and hoping that when I fall off the horse (again) it will be for short periods of time.

Maybe the salve I could smear on our collective hearts is to propose that self-sabotage is a myth. We are animals with intelligence and an evolutionary drive towards self-improvement. Each failure is an instance of adaptation which teaches those who come after us how not to do it, or, at a minimum, how to do it better.

Let's stop the self-flagellation, please. Adding injury to insult is counterproductive. And yes, we are terribly inconsistent, always nurturing the inevitable, insurmountable gap between human ambition and human capacity.

But isn't that wonderful? The fact that we wish for things beyond our current capabilities is beautiful.

And now's your turn: **What are my self-sabotaging behaviors?**

What relationship do I need to repair?

<u>Evelyn, 13 years old</u>: I got into an argument with one of my friends and I never resolved it. I regret not making up with her. I feel sad when I see her. I could make things so much better.

<u>John</u>: I can think of a very close relative and reflect upon our different, far apart lives: our moments of friction and conflict. Our disagreements. Our attempts at reconciliation, and the emotional content that's been accumulated along the way. It's overwhelming, like piles and piles of baggage. I must have kept them in random and distant storage units, and I can't even find the keys. Once in a while, I am reminded about this desolate and sullen space in my mind. I am reminded that I once cared about the relationship. And I ponder what can I do to make it better?

I think good thoughts and wish them well, but know the course of our life relationship could have been different, if only.

Reparation starts with confession. With admitting complicity and expanding mutual compassion. Some wounds can never be mended, but our acceptance can allow the goodwill that remains to take root and grow.

<u>Cristina</u>: This one is easy to answer! Not because repairing relationships is easy, but because I have been working fanatically on this process for more than 20 years. I find this to be one of the most effective pathways to transformation. We can't get where we want to go with broken dynamics hanging around our necks. That slate needs scrutiny and ongoing scrubbing!

When I was in my twenties, I took a blank notebook and at the top of each page I put the name of each person with whom I felt the need to clear something out. From the high school girlfriend that (virtually) stabbed me in the back, to the stepmother I (literally) stabbed in the side with an aluminum fork when I was a kid, plus all the people in between.

If thinking about a given relationship still bothered me as I was looking at that open notebook, it meant that it needed work, and working at it is what I did - a spectacularly effective investment in my mental health.

In some cases, writing the name in that notebook was all that needed doing: acknowledgement! Other times, I had to follow up face to face, and with a select some, it took mutual work.

I cannot express how much space was cleared in my heart and mind by this repair process! A tremendous amount of psychological bandwidth was engaged to manage emotions and histories - energy which, once cleared up, was available for use in other ways.

Ever since, I have learned my lesson, and when murky stuff happens between myself and other humans, I clear the air as fast as I can, owning my role in the tension, and calling them on theirs. Some can face it, some can't, and that's all right. It is what it is, and it takes what it takes.

On rare occasions, I get stuck on something, and the cleaning expedition takes me through endless detours of rumination, self-victimization, and righteousness. I hate the loop-to-loop. I hate the imaginary and thoroughly silly conversations I have in my head. And yet, maybe that's just normal when relationships die and we hurt.

Therapy helps, of course, especially for formative relationships, and particularly if we have baggage with folks who already died. Such complications could add an extra dimension to excavate, but this archaeology of misery is worth doing.

Buy yourself a notebook and find a pen. Best money you've spent in a long while, I guarantee it.

And now's your turn: **What relationship do I need to repair?**

What is the one thing I didn't get to do when I was little, that I can still do today?

<u>Cristina:</u> When I was fourteen, my father used his extraordinary talents and the meager communist supplies at his disposal to give me a very special space of my own. He frescoed the walls with post-modern swirls of stylized butterflies in shades of green and purple (my then favorite color), built a bespoke wall-to-wall bookshelf (purple, of course), lacquered the wooden floors to mirror-perfection, and reupholstered the aging fold-up couch using the same rich fabric as the window coverings. He also came up with the idea of installing a disco ball (tiny mirrors and all). For this, he repurposed a projector lamp from his photo lab, and wired the walls to install a switch and the tiny motor for the disco ball. Only that he could never get the actual disco ball quite right, which left my ceiling with an empty hook.

Fast forward a couple of decades, and for my birthday this year, I asked my husband to install a disco ball in our basement. With delivery and installation, it took about a day.

Once the disco ball went up, I pretended I was 14 again and cranked my favorite playlist, busting moves under the swirling lights. While the first moments were glorious, at the 20-minute mark I was so utterly motion sick I had to leave the room.

Moral of the story? Just because you have been thinking about it since you were a child, doesn't mean that it won't make you throw up today. Don't get me wrong, I am all for following one's dream with ferocious relentlessness, but it is possible that some of them might be better left on paper only.

John: I wish all children were taught to nurture their inner peace.

When I was a child, I was constantly focused on what's next. The "now" was overrun by transactional and experiential aspirations. Stimulation and gratification were on my mind, which of course, is natural for a growing mind. The problem was that nothing seemed to tame my exponentially expanding sense of self-importance. I was stuck in my cranial beehive of self-obsession, anxiety, self-judgment and loneliness.

I can't imagine how today's youth manage to handle this all given the amplification of social media! I was adrift, lost in an overpowering sea of thinking, nurturing some dreams, but most of it was self-mutilation.

I had no tools to manage my thoughts. To regulate my emotions. To overlay perspective on what was on my mind. I did not have the skills to understand that I am not my thoughts.

I blame no one, and have no hard feelings. I now know what inner peace is. How to regulate my breathing and my emotions. How much energy I get from it. I realize that my compassion, empathy, and my sense of connection to others was hibernating, and I yearn for different tools to awaken all who need it.

While I have no regrets, I wish all children are given the tools and opportunities to understand and appreciate themselves plus the beautiful world around them. To be trained in the habit of stillness, of quietly sorting through the noise in their minds to hear the truth of their hearts. This is my childhood wish for all children.

And now's your turn: **What is the one thing I didn't get to do when I was little, that I can still do today?**

What makes me cry?

<u>John</u>: I honestly don't know.

I can cry at the drop of a hat, with tears and a loss of breath, during moments which could seem empty, impulsive, and unpredictable. A movie, a TV commercial, an inspirational story that reaches into my heart - they can all make me cry. Is it guilt, or pent-up emotions?

There is another kind of crying, internal, when I am really at a loss. This hits me when I think of loved ones who have passed, or remember moments when I could have done better as a parent and husband.

I'm learning not to avoid such moments. I confront them. I own them. I grieve them. But it feels like I am holding back an avalanche of tears. Not sure why or how. I want to cry more but I worry I may never stop.

<u>Cash, 14 years old</u>: Seeing my brother struggle with his disability makes me cry. It's not fair that he has to face those challenges, and I wish I could take them away. *

<u>Cristina</u>: Because of my culture of birth, there is bullshit-stoicism and misplaced pride taking center stage in my psyche, so I seldom cry.

What can I say, I am a cold bitch, and more often than I would like to admit, kinda proud of it, because it is useful. Being emotionally cold is protective. It is power. But is it healthy? Sure isn't!

Longitudinally, it is scientifically documented that not crying does shorten one's lifespan. You read that right: people who cry less, live statistically significant shorter lives. Therefore, I am trying to get in touch with my softer side, allowing deep feeling, and giving myself permission to be impacted by small moments of grace or beauty that make me cry with awe, feelings of injustice that make me cry with anger and frustration, and realizations of loss that make me cry with longing and grief.

Feeling is an advanced game.

And now's your turn: **What makes me cry?**

343

What makes me angry?

<u>Luca, 15 years old</u>: I think everyone gets angry when life doesn't go their way. I think this is the definition of being angry. Being angry is normal. The true question is, what level of angry should we allow ourselves to experience?

<u>Tanya, 12 years old</u>: When someone messes with one of my friends, I get angry. When I say "stop" to someone and they don't stop, I get angry. When someone says something to me that is inappropriate, I might get angry. Also, if I am working on a project and it is not going how I want it to go, there is a bit of anger that surfaces, mixed with frustration.

<u>Cristina</u>: Because childhood trauma bestows a really short fuse, lots of things make me angry: time wasted. Ingratitude. Barriers. Sarcasm. Rudeness. Deceit that hits me in the pocket. Mess. Disrespect. Gauche deeds.

I am too often angry at myself, and always angry at the injustice of the world.

But anger is less important than we think, just a weather system pointing to things that need scrutiny and revealing inner truths that shouldn't be denied. What is important is what I do with the anger once it is here. I used to fight it, equating "anger" with "weakness" and unsuccessfully trying to suppress it. I don't do that anymore, not because *"if you can't beat them, join them"* (although maybe that too), but because anger is high octane fuel in one's own engine.

Today I use anger as energy, to clean the house, make course corrections, kick emotional leaches out of my life, and look myself in the eye.

Anger is better than the Ancient Greek Oracle of Delphi, and much less cryptic: anger shows the way.

<u>John</u>: My deepest anger is full of disappointment and reserved for myself. In the end, I can really only control what I do, and when I fail, I have to hold myself accountable. And that angers me. Not out of control anger, hysteria, and the histrionics of a young, idealistic person, but the despair of a wiser person who should know better, and be in sync with what I expect from myself.

And now's your turn: **What makes me angry?**

When am I lonely?

<u>Emery, 17 years old</u>: I feel lonely when I find myself scrolling on my phone for hours, stuck on one line of thought, without other people. It is that kind of stuck-ness where there's just one more thing you can click. This combination brings a bad kind of loneliness, and I see darkness. My brain enters a very specific and very small world, and I can't see the value of my physical and emotional context. In those moments, I should use my phone to call a friend, but that doesn't happen because I'm in the silo, at my loneliest.

<u>John</u>: When I'm deeply missing something: the counsel of my mother, the laughter of a friend I have lost.

I think loneliness is a disturbing, ever-present tone in our minds. We can pay attention to it, or ignore it as it lurks in the shadows of the mind, reminding us that we're by ourselves because we've been orphaned by our parents' death, or by abandonment, or by the lack of companionship in our lives. If we happen to have many dysfunctional relationships in our life, the loneliness compounds, and the volume of that tone in our heads increases.

Hearing the sound of loneliness has no rhyme or reason. I could be in a crowd, I could be surrounded by loving people, I could be immersed in a moment that should be satisfying and happy, then bam! I don't know why it happens, and my vulnerability rises to a discordant, inner symphony. An enigmatic emptiness fills me with dread, I feel inadequate or hopeless, and my deepest loneliness hits. What's ironic, is that I rarely feel lonely when in solitude. When I am truly by myself, I feel connected to my soul, all people, and all things. My practice of solitude has been my "loneliness-noise-cancellation".

<u>Cristina</u>: I never feel lonely. Or I don't know, maybe I have been so lonely all my life that I can't even tell the difference… Either way, the trick is to like one's own company, and to respect what and who one is. Then you have a spectacular companion at all times.

Ego? Perhaps.

Does it matter? You tell me. Would you rather be lonely?

And now's your turn: **When am I lonely?**

How long should I live?

<u>John</u>: I am not sure about the word "should". How long *will* I live? How long *can* I live? And what quality of life might I experience during whatever life expectancy I am given? We all have a hidden expiration date, probably sudden, possibly prolonged, and most likely not in accordance to our timetable.

We are told over and over how precious time is. Not to waste it, to seize the day, etc. But we ignore these inspirational thoughts, and see them as trite admonitions. It's the existence of tragedy which most often reminds us of the brevity and gravity of existence. During such times, we slow down and become a bit more conscious. But memory fades, and we often return to less cautionary habits.

I don't know how much time I should have. Can I truly relinquish expectations about how long my life should be? Probably not. I want to feel a sense of fulfillment if I die right now. I want to know that however long my life, I have given my all every step of the way.

<u>Evelyn, 13 years old</u>: Living to 100 is a good goal. But I don't want to be alive when I can't walk or do anything. When I am suffering more than enjoying life

<u>Cristina</u>: I should live 113 years. Might as well, no? That's the plan, made in concordance with current data on potential human lifespan, plus my gargantuan ambition. Above that, I should live as long as it is meaningful, as long as it is dignified, as long as there's a point to it. If that includes spending time with my potential grandchildren, that's gravy. We'll see.

And now's your turn: **How long should I live?**

When do I feel shame?

<u>Luca, 15 years old</u>: I feel shame when I do something that is "bad", and by that, I mean morally incorrect. We feel it in our gut and in our heart when something is morally incorrect and people also calibrate us regarding what society considers morally incorrect. Drinking alcohol, for example, some people think is morally incorrect, some don't, but either way alcohol is bad for my body. We were talking about self-sabotage earlier; drinking is a prime example.

<u>Tanya, 12 years old</u>: If I accidently say something rude to someone, I feel bad about it. Hurting other people by accident and not by accident, makes me feel embarrassed.

<u>John</u>: Even the word "shame" sends a shiver down my spine, deeply entrenched with nightmarish feelings. Shame is deeper and darker than disappointment or embarrassment, and it lives at the lightless bottom of the emotional ocean. Shame is the rawest of feelings. Grief is brutal, but often in reaction to another's tragedy. Shame strips one down to the most basic properties of our humanity, beneath layers of pretension and performative impressions, under the mask of who we present to the world, and cuts open at the nerve ending between who we are and who we want to be.

I feel this kind of shame when I remember words I shouldn't have said to people I love most. I feel shame thinking about thoughtless, brutally harsh, and unfair things I did in the name of irrelevant, selfish, and egotistical matters. That is my greatest dimension of anguish: that some of my actions were unnecessary.

The only escape I see from the debilitation of shame, is to be propelled to rise to the surface of that emotional ocean, then breathe the oxygen of redemption and renunciation.

<u>Cristina</u>: I am ashamed of being a girl.

Can you believe that? It's not that I want to be something else other than a girl. No. I am simply ashamed of allowing myself to live with the needs and traits of a girl.

In this modern world, being a girl is a liability and second-class citizenry – and I am ashamed. Behaving "like a girl" is frowned upon. And certainly, behaving like a girl while being a girl, feels like the ultimate, unforgivable trespassing, and the most shameful thing I could do.

Stupid? You bet. Absurd? Absolutely! Where does this shame come from? Professional hypotheses abound, but it doesn't matter.

Crying? That's the ultimate sin, because who wants to deal with a crying woman?

Feelings? Fragility? Forget it.

In this world made by men for men, the more normal something is for a girl to do, the more shameful it feels to me. Thus, day in and day out, I turn up the volume on the *Yang* of who I am, rooting out the *Yin* as a cavity. I cultivate my inner masculinity which is rewarded by our capitalist, individualistic, Western narratives. But I am not going to lie, bypassing my femininity is an excision, a renunciation of self; and it hurts. Worse yet, I've got so good, I don't even know I'm doing it.

I hate this charade completely, because *"behaving like a girl"* is something I have been conditioned to avoid at all costs. Excruciating. Exhausting. And plain sad.

As I said, crazy.

I am an incredibly powerful woman inside and outside, so I have been conditioned to curate a more androgynous behavior in all aspects of my life, from design of my home *("can't be too feminine!")* to my clothes *("elegant but it better have some structure")*.

I almost missed out on being a mother because I was ashamed to even say out loud that I wanted to have a baby. Thank God I got over that. Now I am raising a girl who is free from my shame.

And this has helped me start to maybe, possibly, perhaps accept the girl I am.

And now's your turn: **When do I feel shame?**

How do I feel about getting old?

<u>Emery, 17 years old</u>: I'm frustrated that it happens. And I feel that I'm only at the very beginning of this process of getting old. I don't want to lose the person I am. I'm afraid of that moment when most of my life will be behind me. Being a young person is part of my identity. Today I'm someone who can do whatever I might do or whatever is interesting - because I have time. That's what it means to be young. I can paradigm-shift so that growing old looks fine, but I know that as I grow old I might not heal as fast as I do now. I might not be as physically able or vibrant. And I think that must be okay because I'll still be me, as long as I hold on to that, and as long as I save myself.

Perhaps it doesn't really matter what happens to my body because I'll still be doing my thing. Yes, I will become old, whatever that ends up meaning, and I can be okay with that as long as I still do the things that I want to do.

<u>Evelyn, age 13</u>: Sometimes I feel very small. The future feels so far away. Thinking about the future, jobs, college, and marriage. I am still so young

<u>Cristina</u>: I am struggling with this right now; I am not going to sugarcoat it.

Getting old is frustrating, and I am terrified of wasting time because I do not know how much of it is given. Time is a fabulous accountability partner but a merciless slave driver. Time doesn't care.

Also, hurting your ankle while simply stepping towards one's mailbox, or injuring an elbow because I lifted a platter at Thanksgiving is weird. I am not enjoying these particularly humorous-only-in-hindsight aspects of getting older. But I do love, absolutely love the amazing things that getting older brings: the knowledge, the ease of gliding through life that sets in at some point, the wisdom, the cool-cucumber-effect that experience imparts as we acquire enough longitudinal data to conclude that most things are inconsequential. I cherish the way days become more precious, choices become curated in a different way, stuff loses relevance because in truth, some things were never relevant - we just thought they were…

I like, more and more, who I become as the days go by. And that's nice. Now I'll go take my vitamins!

John: For a long time, I looked much younger than my age, and people would make remarks about my youthfulness, which I assumed meant they did not respect or trust me and my qualifications. How is that for a guy who cannot take a compliment and turns victory into defeat?

I used to say I can't wait to have gray hair so that people would respect me more. Be careful what you wish for!

Nowadays, I look at the aging process, and find getting older to be an amazing experience! To accumulate the birthday candles, gray hairs, and wrinkles has been an incredible journey. I've been lucky and privileged, and with the passage of time my life has increasingly improved, both economically and spiritually. My understanding of myself has increased too, and that made me more curious.

And because my health is sound, I don't think the full toll of aging has made its mark. While I know that fragility might be coming sooner than I think, I am able to remind myself how miraculous it is that I'm still here.

And now's your turn: **How do I feel about getting old?**

What is death?

<u>Amber, 7 years old</u>: Death is when someone's body stops working, and they're not alive anymore. It's sad and scary to think about this. My grandparents tell me that we can honor the people who have died by remembering them and living our lives. *

<u>John</u>: An immortal mindset is the cardinal sin because death is just the other side of life. It's the inevitable conclusion to the story. The great certainty of our existence.

Everything that is born dies. All things are impermanent, and this is not something that should be feared. It is part of the truth that we need to live by. How we react to death, how we understand it, will dictate how we actually live.

Ready to go

Always have to be ready to go!
What do we take with us?
What do we have to show?
Leaving is never easy
Our luggage nearly packed
What do we discard?
What do we gift?
To lighten our burden
To enable our shift
The door is always open
Could be any time
But we must be ready

Whether painful or sublime
The moment not ours
Our departure unexpected

but never a surprise

No one knows if anyone cries
The folly of assumptions made
We ponder what could have been
Did we get a passing grade?
Never walk this way again

We forgot
that when we were born, we began to die

The law of averages never applies

Time is in infinite motion
Just a drop in the ocean
No room for regrets we dread
Or of the words unsaid
Time to unpack the baggage

It is getting late

I hear the train coming

My destiny and my fate
This much is true
Life is so short
I am ready to go, are you?

<u>Cristina</u>: Death is absence. Destination. Terminus point. The end of all conversations. The point of no return, the point of no advancement, the point of no repair.

Death is also the successful fulfillment of this human experience. The greatest mystery. The biggest adventure with no preview.

Death should be the most dramatic and meaningful act of existence, because it is anyway. Let's not die like a silent fart from a too-gluttonous meal; let's die like a supernova of everything we have been while alive.

And now's your turn: **What is death?**

For what would I risk everything?

<u>Tanya, 12 years old</u>: I don't know, but probably for my children, in the future.

<u>Cristina</u>: For love. For honor. For my child. For what is right. This is philosophical math I have done long ago, revised at regular intervals, and still found true. It's simple.

<u>John</u>: The answer is not God, country, or family. It's really not.

Instead, I know that I would risk everything for the moment of unexpected truth of word or deed, provoked by something unpredictable, triggered by an instance when we have to lay it all on the line for career, marriage, the welfare of children, or perhaps life itself.

In my mind I am ready to risk everything in that way. But am I?

And now's your turn: **For what would I risk everything?**

If I could start anew, what kind of life would I choose for myself?

<u>Cristina's take on this</u>: I would be fearless in all the ways that matter, and never be embarrassed by my needs, nor consider them weakness.

I would love unconditionally and protect myself less.

I would ask for feedback.

I would waste no time fighting with those I love.

I would not wait for other people to figure out what they want.

I would waste no time ruminating.

I would use money with a bit more wisdom.

I would be gentler. Kinder.

I would enjoy my beauty and femininity without self-judgment.

I would work out every day.

I would put less pressure on myself.

I would exercise my voice as loud and as often as necessary.

And now I go and do all such things because I still can! I can't go back and spend more time with my dead father. I can't go back and get a dog 10 years before I did. I can't reach out into my teenage years and embrace my queerness. I can't be 30 again and have a kid. I can't teleport to 2002 and fly to the edge of space in a MIG, which now is no longer possible. But for some things, there's still time.

<u>John</u>: We can always reinvent ourselves while we're living. It's not easy, but it is possible.

Yes, it's facile and steeped in self-pity to imagine being born anew into some wealthy, more talented, and better-looking container, with a much smoother life and no struggle. But is that what we want?

Jean Paul Satre described how our existence precedes the essence, and we can't know why we are here without actually living. We can't understand the beauty and privilege of running without first falling and scraping the knee. Experience is indeed the teacher of essence.

We can live multiple lives with extraordinarily different chapters across the evolution of our being because we are not sentenced to perpetually stay on the monorail that we're on. We don't have to accept a predetermined destination.

A fresh life is always right in front of our eyes, ripe for the taking if we could only bother to do the necessary work. No one said it would be easy, and yes, maybe the hardest thing we'll ever do is start anew while overcoming the pain of beginning again. But the beautiful flight of becoming can be embraced to reengineer the life we want.

The trick? Regret nothing. Start now.

And now's your turn: **If I could start anew, what kind of life would I choose for myself?**

What now?

Three Calls to Action

1. Reflect on any and all the questions, and on what they stirred in you.
2. Share the questions. Maybe your answers. Discuss with someone.
3. Don't sit on your ass. Act upon the things you discovered.

INDEX

Change

Identity

#10   What brings me joy?

#11   What did I say I wanted to be when I was 5, 10, 15, and
       25 years old?

#12   What makes me, me?

#14   What makes me feel younger?

#15   What is my untapped potential?

#17   When do I feel connected to the universe?

#18   What gives me pleasure?

#21   Where do I come from?

#23   What sacrifices have past generations made in order for
       me to be here?

#24   How am I misunderstood?

#25   What gives me pause?

#39   What luck does play in my life?

#43   What good do others see in me that I don't?

#44   When do I lose the sense of time?

#52   Am I trustworthy?

#53   What gives me peace?

#58   What is my philosophy of life?

#60   What does having kids/not having kids mean to me?

#63   For what will I risk a broken heart?

Goals

Legacy

Path

Pain

#81	What have a learned from my biggest mistake?
#100	What is my biggest regret so far?
#107	When will I apologize?
#109	How can I do less harm?
#110	What are my self-sabotaging behaviors?
#111	What relationship do I need to repair?

Self

#13	What place inspires me?
#19	What is a good life?
#22	Do I trust myself?
#26	What is my relationship with nature and living things?
#27	What answers am I looking for?
#28	What is beauty?
#29	What expectation of me, that others have, interferes with my success?
#30	What is my relationship with money?
#31	What is my need for prestige?
#34	How accurate is my moral compass?

#29   Where does my self-doubt come from?

#37   Why don't I get the credit I deserve?

#38   Why do I feel that I am not enough?

#41   What is true love?

#42   Why do I care so much about what others think?

#45   Could I be generous without expectations?

#46   What does "being busy" mean to me?

#47   What is God to me?

#48   Is there a difference between doing good and being good?

#50   What must it be like to be my adversary?

#54   What form of selfishness have I been practicing?

#56   How can I strengthen my self-love?

#59   What role should my significant other play in my life?

#64   How do I know what's true?

#65   Where in my life do I have complete faith?

#66   In which ways is my life out of balance?

#67   When am I stuck?

#68   Have I paid my dues?

#69   What is my strongest prejudice?

Time